GROWING TREES ON THE GREAT PLAINS

GROWING TREES ON THE GREAT PLAINS

Margaret Brazell

Fulcrum Publishing
Golden, Colorado

Library of Congress Cataloging-in-Publication Data

Brazell, Margaret.
    Growing trees on the Great Plains / Margaret
Brazell.
        p.   cm.
    Includes bibliographical references and index.
    ISBN 1-55591-096-3
    1. Windbreaks, shelterbelts, etc.—Great Plains. 2.
Tree planting—Great Plains. 3. Trees—Great Plains.
I. Title.
SD409.5.B73   1992   91-58488
634.9'5'0978—dc20   CIP

Printed in the United States of America

0 9 8 7 6 5 4 3 2 1

Fulcrum Publishing
350 Indiana Street, Suite 350
Golden, Colorado 80401

7518

To my husband, Bill, with thanks for his hard work in making our trees grow; to our daughter, Bonnie, and future generations, who make it all worthwhile

Contents

Contents

Preface

This book was written because a ranch couple wanted to grow some trees and had a tough time doing it. I'm the ranch woman. I grew up on a ranch nestled among the ponderosa pines of the Black Hills of South Dakota; when I moved with my husband to a ranch on the open plains, I learned about wind. Some days you could almost see it. If there was a breeze among the pines at my parents' house, it was a gale where we lived. These contrasting worlds of fragrant pines and windy plains existed not more than a mile apart.

One particularly dry year I read James Michener's *Centennial*, in which plains women went crazy from listening to the incessant wind. Wind is worst in a dry year, and that's the way it was as I read that book. I could hear it howling, and I knew what it was doing to our chances of a crop. I didn't go crazy, but I could see that it would be possible.

Shortly after taking possession of our land, my husband and I stepped off a spot for our first shelterbelt or windbreak. Its parallel rows of closely planted trees would be positioned at right angles to the prevailing wind to give optimum protection from the elements to our house and barn. This was the start of one of the most optimistic tree-planting projects ever undertaken by this ranch family. When we weren't planting trees, we were scheming about which kind to plant and where. We dug up small pine trees from my parents' land by the pickup load and hauled them home to plant. We studied nursery catalogs. We visited local tree nurseries and wrote big checks for the privilege of bringing home trees that we were certain would astound us with their growth. Within a year we had planted hundreds of trees in the five rows of the shelterbelt northwest of our buildings, 75 pine seedlings, and several rows of Siberian elm around the house. The books said sugar maples were hardy to our zone, so we even tried them.

Those were wonderful years. Our optimism was exceeded only by our ignorance. It was fun to imagine the lofty tops of our shelterbelt trees swaying in the breeze. We would someday tap the sugar maples by the east line fence, and the pines would easily outgrow their sisters left behind in dad's woods. If "effort equals results," we would soon be living in a young forest.

The truth is, for a while we lived around a lot of stunted or dying trees. Our trees didn't look anything like those in the books or nursery catalogs. We put honey on our pancakes because the sugar maples were dead twigs. While the stand of pines from which we had adopted ours was head-high to a tall man, ours were putting out a mere 2 inches of growth a year, barely hanging on despite all the water we gave them. The wind still swept across the plains, whipping the garden, rattling the windows, robbing our crops of moisture, and stressing our livestock.

We finally learned the lessons that enabled us to grow some trees. Gradually, what had been a bare farmstead became surrounded with shelterbelts; our place stands out like a little oasis from the distance. These days we don't think in terms of the number of trees on our ranch but the number of entire shelterbelts.

Now the methods that work well for us seem obvious, and we wonder why we didn't try those first. We also wonder how many other dryland tree growers are wasting time using techniques that were invented and tested somewhere in tall corn country. We dryland tree growers need to plant tree species that are tough enough to survive in this harsh climate, and we need sound practices that have been tried and proven in low rainfall areas similar to our own.

The techniques described in the following chapters have been successful for me in growing trees in western South Dakota. Because our rainfall amounts and general climate are representative of much of the semiarid Great Plains, corresponding results can be expected in similar regions. While urban-dwellers enjoying the favorable micro-climate created by the surrounding city will find these tree-growing methods beneficial, I have primarily focused on practices necessary in the more severe conditions that rural homeowners and ranchers like myself have to cope with in order to grow trees.

Some people call a bucket a pail; some call a sack a bag. The same difference applies to *windbreaks* and *shelterbelts*. When I refer to windbreaks and shelterbelts in this book, I mean one or more rows of trees that protect your home, cattle, garden, or crops from the wind and elements. I like the term windbreak; in my mind I spell it "windbrake" because it's a more accurate description of what a windbreak does. These can vary greatly in size. Some of my shelterbelts are only 350 feet long, whereas I've seen some that stretch for a mile or more on the edge of a field.

Technically, a windbreak could be a wooden fence, too. Since this is a book about trees, you can be safe in assuming that I'm talking about rows of trees.

I will also refer to a *tree planting*. This is a much broader term than shelterbelt or windbreak. Not all trees are planted in neat rows. Some are grouped in a wet spot made where a dam seeps, while others may be single trees grown in a pasture for cattle shade or near a driveway for automobile shade. When I refer to a tree planting, I mean every type of arrangement, from a single tree or row to multiple-row shelterbelts. Tree planting in this book means trees you plant anywhere.

CHAPTER ONE

Land of Torrential Dry Spells

"Son, our dry spells can best be described as torrential."
> —*North Dakota resident, quoted by Philip Hamburger*

Library shelves sag with the weight of tree books. The trouble is, most of these seem to be written in the shade of oak trees rooted in 30 feet of topsoil with the water table at 7 feet. They are written by people who have experience growing trees in the humid, well-watered areas of the country where, if farmers don't faithfully keep tree seedlings out of pasture and farmland, they will return to the predominantly wooded state in which their ancestors found them.

I grow trees in a less favorable environment, however. Western South Dakota—like the semiarid plains of Canada and the dry plains from North Dakota to Texas—is not so fortunate to boast topsoil measured in yards. In general, it is the 100th meridian that marks the transition from wet and humid to semiarid in North America. To the east of this meridian lies land which flourishes under the plow. To the west of the 100th meridian lie the drought-prone plains where grass is king. It is this unique part of the continent that this book is directed toward.

Mother Nature seems to have intended grass and forbs to grow in semiarid environs, and she does a wonderful job. She lines the creek banks and spring-fed draws with trees, but out on the open plains she puts grass: buffalo grass, green needle grass, blue grama, sideoats grama, bluestem, a variety of wheat grasses, and a few tough broadleaf plants such as wild sunflower, fringed sage, yucca, and prickly pear cactus. Leave farmland alone, and it reverts to grass not trees. In areas of more plentiful rainfall there is a struggle between grass and forest for dominance, but that competition simply does not exist naturally on the plains. There is no question that grass is going to win out. You'll not find farmers grubbing volunteer tree seedlings out of pastureland where nature's idea is to grow grass.

On the other hand, where nature takes a notion to put trees in a drought-prone region, she has little trouble growing them. The ponderosa pine–covered Black Hills rising from the treeless plains of western South Dakota create a striking contrast between grassland and forest. On our plains, trees mark the course of the creeks; snakes of green meander from the Black Hills to the Missouri River. No doubt there are numerous oases of trees throughout the semiarid quarters of the Great Plains; the problem is that they don't always grow as easily where they will do the most good. Nature can grow a pine tree out of a crack in a granite boulder in the Black Hills, whereas I labor and sweat to make one grow in reasonably tillable soil.

2

Dryland Territory

The maps in Figures 1.1 and 1.2 show mean annual precipitation for certain Canadian cities and for climatic regions in the United States. Generally, those areas of the plains receiving less than 18 inches, or 450 mm, of total precipitation are definite candidates for the dryland tree-growing techniques discussed in this book. Some mountainous sites also receive less than 18 inches of precipitation, but their alpine nature demands unique cultural methods not covered here. Areas outside of the Great Plains, yet similar in climate and growing conditions, would also benefit from these dryland tree-growing methods.

The dryland area to which I refer as *the plains* covers much of the mid-United States between the Rocky Mountains and the 100th meridian, reaching from southwestern Texas to the Canadian border. In Canada, the dryland region includes the southern grasslands of the provinces of Alberta, Saskatchewan, and Manitoba.

Factors other than total moisture are also important in determining dryland territory. For instance, warmer regions experience greater evaporation than those in the cooler north; thus 18 inches of precipitation in Texas may not be equal to 18 inches in North Dakota in terms of how much moisture will be available to a tree. Grasses grow well with 14 inches of moisture on the northern plains, but 17 inches is required in eastern Colorado and 21 in northern Texas in order for the plants to have the same amount of water available for growth. Greater heat produces greater evaporation from the plant itself and from the soil. Timing

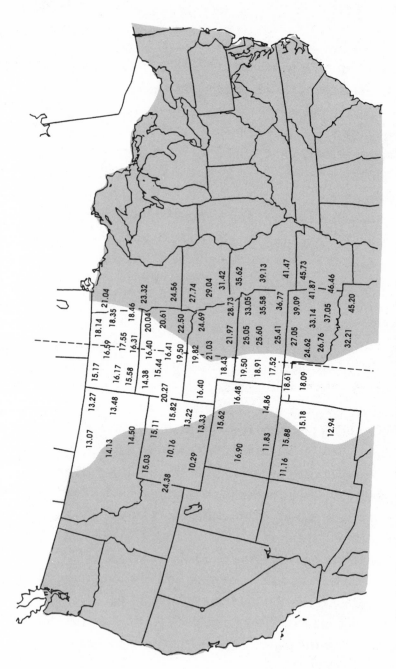

Fig. 1.1. Average annual U.S. precipitation amounts for the Great Plains. Source: Climatic Atlas of the United States. Asheville, N.C.: National Climatic Data Center, June 1968 (U.S. Department of Commerce, National Oceanic and Atmospheric Administration).

of the precipitation is also important, because that which falls during the growing season is available to the tree when it needs it the most and is not subject to evaporation before the plant needs it.

Bear in mind that the precipitation amounts of Figures 1.1 and 1.2 are averages over many years. The particular spot you have chosen for planting a tree may receive considerably more or less than that listed for your region. For example, Rapid City, South Dakota, averages 16 inches of moisture per year, while 12 to 14 inches per year are more realistic amounts near our ranch, even though we are a mere 25 miles from Rapid City.

Similarly, soils differ, water tables vary immensely, and rainfall patterns produce both favorable and unfavorable microclimates locally. For example, clusters of springs and high water tables create pockets of paradise amid miles of dry prairie and enable moisture-loving species to thrive. River and creek drainages also produce a different tree-growing situation from that found on surrounding high ground, even though the two settings may be within sight of each other. Major water drainages, in effect, receive more moisture than the precipitation maps of Figures 1.1 and 1.2 indicate, creating microclimates that can grow trees more easily than surrounding dryland plains. The techniques described in this book would also be useful in growing trees on subirrigated bottomland, however, because the moisture levels in the upper layers of bottomland soil are similar to that on upland prairie. Tree roots must find moisture in the top few feet of soil during their first years. The water that exists 10 feet below doesn't do them much good until several years later.

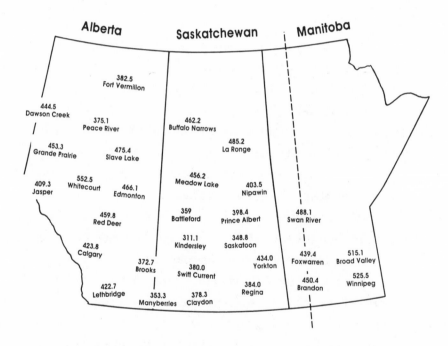

Fig. 1.2. Average annual Canadian precipitation amounts in millimeters. Source: Canadian Climate Normals: 1951-1980. Downsview, Ontario: The Climate Control Program of the Atmospheric Environmental Service, 1982.(Map by Susan Hunt.)

Dryland Conditions

To a tree, the most important feature of our plains climate is that we don't have average years. We have extremes. A dry blast of summer wind may parch everything in the space of a few days and continue to develop into a decade-long drought. On the other hand, a warm, moist body of air from the Gulf of Mexico may collide with a cold, low-pressure front out of the Rockies and dump 6 inches of rain overnight. Such extremes are far from unusual.

It would be safe to say that the weather where I live is usually record-breaking. We often seem to be on the edge of one weather extreme or another. The weather forecasters here tend to speak in terms of the driest/hottest/windiest/coldest month or year since the all-time driest/hottest/windiest/coldest instance since the early years of record-keeping.

Record high rainfall in Rapid City, for example, is 27.47 inches in 1982, and the record low rainfall is 7.51 inches in 1936. Such swings in moisture levels limit the growth of plants, making this short grass country, and require an approach to tree growing that recognizes the harshness of the climate. Statisticians can average rainfall, but trees cannot.

Wetland Advice and Dryland Conditions

We who struggle to keep a tree alive on scant rainfall, in less than ideal soil, fall through the cracks of prevailing tree-growing approaches. Guidance on how to grow a tree where even nature doesn't is difficult to find. Often, suggestions aimed at high rainfall areas are worthless in dry country. For instance, while you can control weed growth with grass sod in an area that gets 40 inches of rain, you cannot grow trees and sod together on 12 inches of moisture.

Shelterbelts, or windbreaks, on dry sites are often planted with rows too close together and trees too closely spaced within the row because specifications for wetter areas were used. In high rainfall regions, tree roots would have reached water by the time canopy growth, or mature tree crowns, would prevent further mechanical tilling of the soil around trees to remove weeds and grasses. In dry country, when cultivation is stopped because tree branches slap the tractor driver in the face, the roots are far from reaching the water table. Furthermore, they are planted so close together that the available moisture from snow and rainfall is simply inadequate to support such a dense tree population.

It's tough for a dense stand of trees to compete against grass and weeds for 12 to 14 inches of rain a year. Wetland approaches employed under dryland conditions don't work. Trees die. If the tree planter had realized this and planted her trees farther apart, she could have cultivated the ground for many more years and extended the effective life of the shelterbelt. In many cases, when cultivation stops and the weeds and grasses move in, the trees experience additional moisture stress, and the shelterbelt gradually declines.

An example of the competition factor is a shelterbelt that my father planted in 1955. I remember handing him the seedlings one at a time from a bucket. It was laid out in the officially recommended row widths, which proved to be too close together as the planting matured. During its youth, when Dad cultivated between the five rows, the trees and bushes thrived. My brother and I picked pails full of sand cherries from the shrub row and brought bouquets of lilacs home every spring. This shelterbelt enjoyed many advantages: it was planted on level land in a reasonably good location and its roots encountered fertile, loamy soil. Despite these advantages, when canopy growth made cultivation physically impossible, the entire shelterbelt went into a slow but steady decline. Gradually, weeds and grass covered the entire shelterbelt and competed with the remaining trees for the available moisture.

The first trees to go were the water-loving cottonwoods, then the more shallow-rooted shrubs. What is left now is a good study of hardy, tough trees. I take into account what has survived in that shelterbelt when I consider what varieties to plant on our own land. Eastern red cedar, Siberian elm, Manchurian apricot, Siberian peashrub, and a few Russian olives are all that remain. Had the shelterbelt been planted in wider rows, it would be a denser stand of trees now and better able to do the job for which it was intended because it could have been cultivated much longer. Now only extensive renovation could rehabilitate it to usefulness.

Providing poor tree-growing recommendations to people in a forested region such as Ohio would not cause such terrible results because trees generally grow well in Ohio whether man helps or not. Giving incorrect suggestions to a plains dryland tree planter results in a greater percentage of dead trees. The trees lose and the grass wins. There is precious little tree-planting activity going on here in the first place, and it's a shame when even those few attempts fail because of misinformation and poor methods.

Dryland Advice

Old-timers tell me that the pioneer woman and her husband who lived on our ranch during the settlement of this country grew lilacs around their house. The house they built has been long gone and so have the lilacs. In fact, no trace of Mrs. White and her husband exist on the ranch they called home except a name on the abstracts. I wish she had planted a cedar or a pine instead of lilacs; a tougher tree might have survived the ravages of 50 years of South Dakota weather. I would like to have a tree that she planted. A gnarled cedar, with trunk and branches shaped by wind and time, would speak volumes to me about endurance and the cyclical nature of things.

I want trees we plant this year to live long after we're gone. I want generations that will follow on this ranch to say, "Those are the trees that Grandma and Grandpa planted way back in '72." One hundred years from now cattle should still be able to seek shelter from the wind behind our pine trees. That's not too much to ask. To grow trees with any other time frame in mind is a waste of effort and resources.

Plant with the Driest Year in Mind

The driest year should be the lowest common denominator in a tree-grower's plan. Trees do not average moisture from year to year like the weatherman does. If a tree cannot survive a year in which 7 inches of precipitation falls, it will not be there to thrive in the 20-inch year. You need to pick the right type of tree, plant it in as favorable location as possible, and care for it as if it will only rain 8 inches a year for the next 10 years.

Drought hasn't been invented in our lifetime. It's been part of the plains for eons. Core samples taken of trees near Slim Buttes, South Dakota, indicate that cycles of drought have been common for centuries. Figure 1.3 is a plot of a tree-ring index for a tree that began life in 1624; the sample was taken in 1979, a span of 355 years. An index of 1.0 indicates near normal tree-ring growth, values greater than 1.0 indicate very favorable tree-ring growth, and values less than 1.0 represent poor tree-ring growth and likely drought conditions.

This index shows that periods of drought are just as normal as wet years. We commonly compare current droughts with those of the 1930s, but the Slim Buttes tree experienced dry periods of much greater depth and duration than the 1930s. The dry years aren't going away just because we want them to. Drought is a reality we have to cope with.

Beware the "Johnny Appleseed" Approach

John Chapman, alias Johnny Appleseed, was a historic figure famous for his commitment to planting apple trees in frontier Pennsylvania and Ohio. He's one of my heroes because he saw the need for trees and he planted them. Johnny grew trees from seeds left in the pumice from cider presses, and maintained seedling nurseries from which he would transplant trees in surrounding territory. His practice was to remain in one area only long enough to plant his trees, construct protection from animals, and provide initial main-

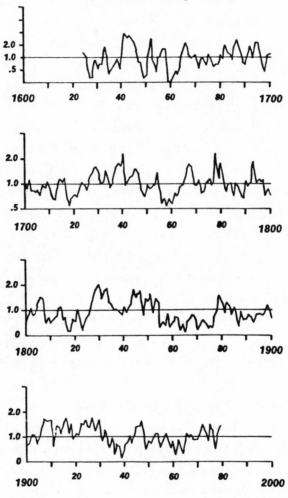

TREE RING INDEX
SLIM BUTTES, SD

Lat. 45°22′, Long. 103°08′

Fig. 1.3. Tree Ring Index: Slim Buttes, S.D. Reprinted with permission from David Meko, Tree-Ring Laboratory, University of Arizona. (Graph by Jim Miller.)

tenance. Because he grew trees in an area that received ample rainfall, he could move on to new settlements and know that his trees would continue to thrive without him.

Johnny Appleseed's methods would have failed completely on the dry plains where I grow trees. He wouldn't have been able to plant trees and abandon them here. When you plant trees in this ecosystem, you are going against the forces of nature. Nature appears to want grass here, not trees; it's going to take effort on your part to win against a system that has been successful for thousands of years. If you simply plant a tree and let nature do the rest, likely as not she'll favor grass over your tree every time. The care you give the tree is the edge that it needs to survive in an environment that is pro-grass.

Such care is a great deal of work but a commitment that you must make for many years if your tree plantings are to succeed. Lack of care is the biggest reason for failure of tree plantings; tree neglect is a waste of the cost of the tree, your work, and resources. You wouldn't think of buying a baby calf and turning it out into a pasture alone, hoping it will be lucky enough to steal some milk from a cow. You wouldn't use this method for raising calves; why raise trees that way?

Plant Only What You Can Care For

Good intentions don't grow trees. I should know. For me the problem typically begins during a January snowstorm. I see a need for more trees, and nursery catalogs beckon me with promises of towering honeylocusts and dense evergreens. After a beastly day out in the driving snow, it is satisfying to fill out large orders for trees to be delivered in April.

Even when the bundle of trees arrives in spring, the soil is usually mellow and moist, and planting them is a joy. A wonderful feeling of accomplishment floods over me as I survey the tidy rows. The soil is freshly tilled, so no weeds mar my glow of pride.

April turns into May, and I manage to give a few doses of water to each tree between spring work and branding. The pace quickens as April and May turn into the hectic days of summer. When I finally have a free moment and venture out to see my trees, I am shocked by how they look. For one thing, I didn't provide water to just the trees; a healthy stand of weeds is making excellent use of it too. Pigweed with fat seed heads crowds around the trees; creeping jenny, or field bindweed, is twining up the tiny trunks; some trees I actually have to search for. I set to work furiously to make up for my neglect. Much damage has already been done by the weeds sapping moisture that the trees will need in the coming months. I vow not to let a single weed grow near a tree again.

I have found that it is better to plant one row of trees and care for them so well that they thrive than to plant the whole 40 acres and have a miserable few survive. In the long run, it is less work to grow a small number well than to fail on a large scale. Faithful care is critical during the early years of a planting, and the most time should be allotted during that period.

CHAPTER TWO

Water Collection Systems

When you plant trees you are making an investment of time, effort, money, and other resources. A tree planting's protection can increase weight gains and profits in your livestock, lower feed requirements, decrease mortality during calving or lambing, decrease home heating costs, protect crops and soil, and increase the market value of your property. If those enhanced benefits and profits can be realized several years sooner, then the savings will pay for the cost of caring for the trees.

The key to early enjoyment of these savings is establishing trees quickly and encouraging their rapid growth. The chapters that follow will be devoted to the aspects of tree culture that are absolutely critical to their success in a dryland setting. Since water is the main limiting factor, much attention needs to be paid to making as much of it available to the tree as possible. In this chapter we'll see how to use various collection methods to bring natural precipitation to the tree. Chapter 3 will aim at preserving that moisture through minimization of competition and evaporation. Chapter 4 recognizes that all of these tricks may not be enough and discusses ways to boost tree survival in the early years of a planting through additional watering. Chapter 5 gives you a profile of the kinds of drought resistant, hardy trees that I have found to thrive. Finally, I'll discuss acquiring stock, planting techniques, and keeping shelterbelts in good condition throughout their life span.

The Problem: Water

The element that restricts tree growth on these semi-arid plains is water. Whatever amount is going to fall from the sky this year is what I have to work with in growing my trees. Many years that amount is not enough for trees to flourish. When nature does not provide enough precipitation, you have to conserve and enhance the moisture that does fall in order for your trees to thrive.

Trees need nutrients from the soil, water, and air to combine with sunlight to complete photosynthesis. Such variables as temperature, humidity, and altitude have to be within the range that the species will tolerate. Where I grow trees we have plenty of sunshine, the air is reasonably clean, and I select trees that will tolerate the extremes in temperature that we enjoy.

Soil quality can be a limiting factor in tree growth on the plains, but even this is correctable and not as detrimental as lack of water. For instance, some soils are underlain with hardpan, a layer of soil close to the surface that cannot be penetrated by water or roots. Often these soils are highly alkaline. Hardpan can be broken up with deep tillage, and alkaline-tolerant species such as Russian olive and Siberian elm survive in this soil. Northern plains soils are adequately fertile to support tree growth; cool temperatures and dryness preserve humus in the soil that burns up in hotter climates. Nutrients are not leached below the root zones by excess rainfall. The main problem with our soils, however, is that often they are just too dry.

You can't make it rain extra inches on your trees, but you can trap some additional moisture and then conserve it so that the trees can obtain all they need. Everything a dryland tree grower does is aimed at enhancing the moisture conditions of the trees. Water is so valuable to plant life on the plains that sneaky thieves, called weeds, employ every tactic to steal what little rainfall exists. The plan is twofold: trap the water and keep it safe for use by your trees.

The Thief: Weeds

Weeds are the foe of successful tree culture. Weed seed numbers in the soil are high: tens of millions per acre in the top 3 inches of soil. Weeds adapt extremely well to the harsh environment of the plains, and they produce enough seed not only for the next year but for many more after that. Many are programmed to germinate at different time intervals. If the weed seed crop is a failure, there are millions more in storage in the soil. Allowing weeds to go to seed where you intend to plant trees adds to the potential weed problem for years to come.

In 1879 botanist William Beal buried 20 jars, each filled with 1,000 weed seeds. Every five years he dug up a jar and planted the contents, his colleagues continuing his work after his death. In 1979 they watched some 100-year-old seeds germinate. That's depressing news for tree growers.

Perennial weeds are even more tenacious than mere seed-producing annuals. Canadian thistle, field bindweed, and leafy spurge are just a few of the noxious perennial weeds that may be a problem for you. These are particularly difficult to eradicate because they are capable of spreading and reproducing by underground runners as well as by seed. They store food reserves in their extensive root systems, so they can survive drought, herbicides, and cultivation better than any weed has a right to.

Nature has a penchant for keeping soil covered. She hates for it to be exposed to the erosive elements and hastens to cover it up with the quickest thing at hand, weeds. Weeds are the tools that nature uses to protect cleanly cultivated land until she can get things back to normal with grass. Weeds are nature's emergency Band-aid™ for bare soil, evidence of nature continuing to do what has worked well for millions of years. You're going against the forces of nature by planting and growing trees. That means you're battling weeds. Remember that in a shelterbelt grass is also a weed.

You cannot grow weeds and trees in the same spot. Weeds occupy space, use available sunlight, and require the same valuable nutrients that your fledgling trees do. Even worse, they compete fiercely for the available water. Lest you think that weeds cannot consume all that much moisture, consider that a full stand of weeds consumes 1/4 to 1/3 inch of moisture per day. An extension service conservation tillage fact sheet informs us that, in growing from 2 to 6 inches, a full stand of *Amaranthus retroflexus*, aptly known as pigweed, uses a little over 1 inch of water. The extension service people apparently don't have the heart to tell us how much water it takes to grow them to seed-bearing maturity. Do you have an inch of water to spare, and have you seen pigweed grow only 6 inches tall given the opportunity?

Where do those weeds get that water? Anywhere they want to. Cocklebur, for instance, roots to an unbelievable depth of over 9 feet and has a potential feeding diameter of 14 feet. Pigweed roots to a mere 8-foot depth and attains a 6-foot diameter. Creeping jenny, that darling of the weed patch, can spread its roots to a diameter of 17 to 18 feet and to a depth of 18 to 20 feet in just three seasons. Compare this to the size of the root structure on those tree twigs you plant in spring. That's one reason the weeds easily grow to 4 feet by August while your trees only put out 8 inches of growth. Many times I've thought that it would be wiser to cultivate the weeds and pull the trees because the weeds seemed to be doing better.

Summerfallow

If you could store several years' worth of precipitation in the soil before you plant your trees, they would have a much better chance of survival. This is exactly what is accomplished by the practice of summerfallow. Competing grass, weeds, alfalfa, or crop growth are killed by tillage so that the moisture these plants would normally use is stored in the soil instead. The decaying vegetation increases the nutrients and organic matter in the soil and in turn improves its water holding capacity, aeration, and the ease with which roots will be able to penetrate in search of moisture. By the time you are ready to plant trees, the soil should be moist and free of competing growth.

Summerfallow not only eliminates annual weeds and many perennial ones but also reduces weed crops in subsequent years by depleting the seed supply. Usually a year of summerfallow is sufficient to kill annual weeds, but perennial ones can require two or even three years. In our area, field bindweed, or creeping jenny, is our most noxious perennial weed. After only one year of summerfallow, this weed appears to do better than ever. If I plant trees after one year of cultivation, the bindweed growth simply explodes the following year. Two years of tillage does a better job of eliminating this and other perennial weeds.

Unless tenacious perennial weeds are present, one year of summerfallow is sufficient. The exception is when the fallow year is abnormally dry and no moisture is accumulated in the soil. One of the main purposes of summerfallow is to store moisture; if none has been available to store, then it is best to wait another year before planting trees. When you do finally plant, your trees will have better moisture reserves to draw on.

If you plan to plant trees on land that is presently growing alfalfa, your site will especially benefit from lying fallow for a year or more because deep-rooted alfalfa, like bindweed, requires considerable cultivation before it is killed completely. Alfalfa is an excellent forage plant, but it is a weed when it flourishes at the expense of a tree.

Summerfallow on Erosive Soils

There is no problem leaving medium to heavy soils bare for a season or two; however, the wind can erode sandy soil without cover. Here's the dilemma: disturb the existing vegetation and expose the soil to wind erosion or let the weeds or grass continue depleting moisture that should be stored for future trees. You can't allow your soil to blow away, but your trees won't have a good chance of survival if they don't have some extra moisture.

Several alternatives are available to deal with this problem: either slow the wind or kill the vegetation without removing it from the soil surface. The best approach may be to do both.

A snow fence erected on the windward side of the planting site will slow the wind considerably and probably keep the soil from blowing. The fence will also create snow drifts where the trees will eventually be planted; this will give an even greater boost to the moisture stored in the soil for the trees. Also a very moist soil won't blow away as easily. It's a good idea to install a snow fence along the windward edge (or the side which takes the brunt of the prevailing wind) of a future shelterbelt site a year or two before tree planting even when blowing soil does not demand it. The site will benefit from the extra moisture.

Herbicides can be used to kill vegetation so that precipitation can be stored without tillage causing erosion. I don't advocate the use of herbicides, but this method will prevent wind erosion while still preparing the site for future tree growth.

If you prefer to till, leave the land surface as rough as possible. Although the rougher surface exposes more soil to the air and dries it out faster, coarse soil particles are less apt to blow away. Repeated disking breaks up clods and leaves the soil more likely to blow away. Plowing leaves the soil in large clumps that are less likely to erode but inverts the clumps so that the vegetation is underneath and unable to help stop wind erosion. Chisel plowing, on the other hand, works the soil deeply and encourages water penetration while leaving the vegetation on top of rough ground where it can protect soil.

The goal of summerfallow is to preserve as much moisture as possible while eliminating weeds and grasses from the planting site. Summerfallow is a work-saver. It lessens the need for irrigation and weed control after the trees are planted. Don't neglect it.

Water-Catching Systems

Water takes the path of least resistance when it runs off the land surface. It seeks the nearest low spot and drains into that area, giving plants there a boost in available moisture. We wisely plant trees in these naturally moist locations. When a favorable site does not exist where we need a tree, we can create one. Your shovel and plow can be your best watering tools if you use them to create water-collecting systems for your trees.

Contoured Hillsides

An exceptionally effective way to collect water for your trees is to contour a hillside to keep rainfall from running off to the valley. Trees are planted in the low area of the contour to take advantage of the extra runoff. If the area is large enough, entire rows of trees can be planted, allowing room to disk on either side.

Contouring is done with large equipment, so this is probably not a do-it-yourself project. If major earthmoving is going to be done, it should be finished enough in advance of tree planting so that the soil has time to settle and make a firm home for tree roots. Weed control must still be practiced on the disturbed soil; otherwise, any gain in moisture will be negated by weed growth.

Dead Furrows

A similar water-catching method for a row of trees is to plant them in a dead furrow. By making one pass with a plow, a slab of sod, or tilled soil, 12 to 18 inches wide is tipped over next to where it originally lay, leaving a long ditch in its place. Its depth depends on how deep the plow is socked into the earth; a furrow 6 to 10 inches deep collects enough extra moisture to be of real value to the trees planted in the bottom of the furrow. The furrow should be plowed just prior to planting because chemical weed control is the only practical way to eliminate water-sapping weeds in the furrow before the seedlings are in place. After planting, other weed control methods, such as mulching, can be used.

A furrow made on the contour of a hillside will collect runoff from the terrain above it; one made in a lowland distributes runoff. Major earthmoving projects like land contouring use the same principles of controlling runoff water to benefit crops, but plowing a dead furrow is within the capability of nearly everyone. Even if you don't own a

Fig. 2.1. Seedling planted in a saucer or basin.

plow, it would be possible to get a strip plowed by a helpful neighbor.

Saucers and Soil Dams

For trees not being grown in a row, a saucer is a good way to provide extra water to the tree. A saucer is a basin surrounding a tree that is dug lower than the rest of the land surface. The saucer should be shaped like an inverted cone, with the tree growing in the middle so that rainfall is directed toward the tree's roots and runoff is held in the basin. (See Figure 2.1.) Such basins, created by water action or animals, exist naturally on plains grassland. A natural depression in the earth that collects water may not exist exactly where you want a tree, but you can duplicate one anywhere.

A saucer collecting water for the tree in its center need not be deep to be effective. You will need to remove only

Fig. 2.2. Seedling planted with soil dam built around it.

enough sod to create a basin a few inches deep. Deeper than this is not necessary and may be detrimental in clay soils or in high-rainfall microclimates. For example, if you are planting on hardpan or heavy soils where drainage is slow, a basin may serve to deliver too much water to the tree planted in its center. Likewise, if your tree is planted where an overabundance of water collects naturally or from irrigation, lowering the planting level even further would be detrimental because too much water cuts off the oxygen supply to the roots, essentially drowning the tree.

In these situations, it would be wiser to build a soil dam around the tree. A soil dam, or low dike, is not lower than the land surface. (See Figure 2.2.) Instead, you build up an earthen dam in a radius around the tree or on the lower side of a tree planted on a hill. A soil dam also collects water, especially that which may run off a hillside. The dam makes irrigating the tree easier as well because it holds water near the tree. However, in the event of long-standing water that can eventually destroy roots, you can easily break the dam down. Later you can rebuild it. If the tree you are planting is surrounded by irrigated lawn, a temporary dike or soil dam is sufficient. A tree planted in a saucer, distant from a garden hose, is seldom in danger of drowning in a semiarid location.

Digging the saucer and building the soil dam is shovel work unless you have better equipment than I do. While building a soil dam does not disturb tree roots, digging a basin after a seedling is planted may. If you dig only a small-diameter saucer at planting time and plan to enlarge it later, you are apt to injure feeder roots, thus doing more damage than good. The best plan is to remove the sod in a large circle and dig an adequate water-catching saucer before a tree is even planted. This way initial watering is a snap, and the tree is able to benefit from any water the basin can collect throughout the growing season.

The diameter of the saucer or soil dam should be at least 3 to 4 feet, though a broader basin is even better. The size of my digging projects is usually limited by my energy and the condition of the soil. The entire saucer area should be mulched; otherwise, weeds will enjoy the extra moisture as much or more than the tree. This is one way to get a tree "set" for a length of time; when other work takes your attention away from trees, something still is working for you.

Snow Traps

Some years a great deal of the moisture on the northern and central plains falls in the form of snow. The actual

WIND   DIRECTION

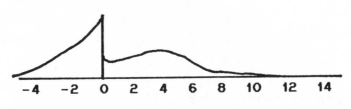

BARRIER: 100% SOLID

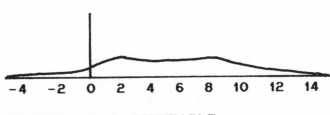

BARRIER: 50% PERMEABLE

*Fig. 2.3. Pattern of snow storage in relation
to barrier density.*

amount of moisture in snow varies considerably; some
contains the equivalent of 1/2 inch of rainfall per 6 inches of
snow while drier snow needs to pile up a foot or more to
equal this amount. The degree of soil-moisture recharge by
snowfall depends on how much frost is in the ground before
it falls, the amount of wind accompanying it, and how fast
it melts. Frozen ground admits little melting snow, and it
often runs off in early spring to fill stock dams and swell
creeks. Such snowmelt is not lost by any means, since it
recharges ground water. It still hurts to see it run away

knowing how dry July can be. On the other hand, wonderfully wet, spring snows melt slowly on thawed ground and soak in to provide a subsoil reservoir of moisture far into the growing season. Snowmelt is not enough to make a crop or grow a tree, but it helps plants survive a drought later in the season.

If you can catch great drifts of snow for your trees, you will be adding several inches of moisture to their yearly allotment. To do this you must understand the behavior of snow and wind. All snow needs is an obstacle to slow the wind and its flakes will fall in a drift. The nature of the obstacle determines its efficacy as a snowflake-tripper. Barriers that are 100 percent solid create turbulence near the barrier and are not effective drift makers; obstacles of 50 percent to 75 percent porosity steal the snow from the wind and drop it in their lee. (See Figure 2.3.)

Snow Fence

Snow fence makes use of this optimum 50 percent to 75 percent porosity to maximize drift formation. Snow fences installed on the upwind side of a tree planting will

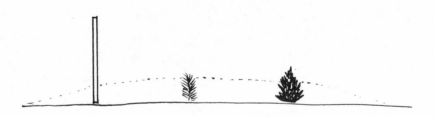

Fig. 2.4. Pattern of snow drift for small trees with a snow fence.

drop deep drifts in their lee and give a free watering to the trees growing nearby. (See Figure 2.4.) Snow fences are particularly valuable in the early years of a tree planting because there is usually nothing else to cause the snow to drop onto the tree rows; the trees themselves are still too small to do the job, and the newly established seedlings have an especially critical need for a steady supply of moisture. As they grow and present a more dense obstacle to the wind, they should become their own snow trap. I'll discuss this more in detail a little later.

Snow fences come in wooden slat variety and in plastics of varied weights, heights, and prices. Plastic lasts the longest, since it resists decay and weathering, and it is available in a wide range of porosities and sizes. In 1988, wooden slat fencing was $23 per 50-foot roll when it went on sale in October, the only time I ever buy it. It is possible to buy it more cheaply at farm sales, especially in corn country where it is used as cribbing.

Fifty-foot rolls of snow fence suddenly seem only 10 feet long when one is putting it up along the north row of a 1/2-mile shelterbelt. For such large areas it may not seem economical, but the cost of the investment in snow fencing should be balanced against the more rapid establishment of the shelterbelt. Extra moisture in these early years will yield benefits over the life of the shelterbelt. You will have a better survival rate, eliminating the cost and labor of replacing dead trees the next year. Better survival will make a solid, continuous wall of trees. This makes for a much more efficient windbreak because gaps in the rows decrease its wind-slowing capability. The good establishment of roots and greater top growth will allow the tree to put out even more growth in subsequent years. The result will be a windbreak that quickly reaches the height and density at which it will begin to protect your cattle, home, or garden.

Living Snow Fence

A row of shrubs that has a lot of foliage and branches near ground level also is an excellent snow-catching barrier. This technique is used especially in shelterbelts. The first row of a multi-row shelterbelt is usually composed of shrubs dense at ground level in order to prevent wind from whistling around the bare trunks of taller trees in the other rows. Its primary purpose is to stop wind at ground level and to initiate immediate snow-dropping action of the shelterbelt. This row drops the bulk of the snow in the space between the windward row and the second row, consequently trapping moisture for the trees, while keeping snow out of the leeward area where your cattle and buildings are. Figure 2.5 is a side view of a typical five-row

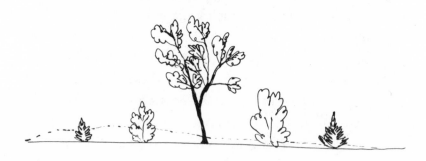

Fig. 2.5. Pattern of snow storage in a five-row shelterbelt.

shelterbelt showing how the windward row traps snow within the trees.

The windward row (the row which faces the prevailing wind) should contain the shrubs able to withstand the weight of snowdrifts because they will take the brunt of the wind's force and the snow burden. The weight of snow has sufficient power to pull down entire fences as it melts; tree branches are even more vulnerable. Shrubs, such as wild plum or buffaloberry, have many branches at ground level, and they are not easily broken when snow forces their boughs to the ground. Cedar or juniper, on the other hand, are often damaged by snow; their central, tallest shoots, or leaders, break when heavy, wet snow piles up on them. Limber deciduous shrubs, like lilacs and honeysuckles, simply spring back into shape after the snow melts. Cedar or juniper can be used in a windward row, but some snow damage can be expected. A broken center leader hurts only the appearance of a cedar; its dense branches at ground level still make an effective windbreak. Wild plum, chokecherry, Siberian peashrub, honeysuckle, Eastern red cedar, and Rocky Mountain juniper are especially good.

An unbroken row of dense bushes in the windward row of a shelterbelt is critical to the success of the other rows of the planting. If the windward row has gaps where trees or shrubs have died out, the rest of the shelterbelt is in jeopardy. The snow-catching system breaks down. For this reason, replace any shrubs or trees that have died after the first growing season but pay special attention to the windward row.

While the windward row of a multi-row shelterbelt drops the bulk of the snow within the first rows, the other rows also help deposit snow, both within the shelterbelt and farther downwind. Tall trees are used in the center rows to provide height to the shelterbelt needed to give good wind protection farthest downwind or leeward. The taller these trees grow, the greater the distance leeward that benefits from reduced wind speed.

Often one tall row is a fast-growing species that provides snow-stopping action quickly while the slower-growing varieties still poke along. Fast-growers are usually shorter-lived so that their row will eventually die out or be removed to allow the slow-growing trees room to mature.

For example, the Siberian elm is a great, drought-tolerant, fast-growing tree, with a life span of 30 to 40 years even here on the plains. I call it a valuable tree. Planted with the slower-growing pine, the elm can be removed when the pine reach a height that will provide protection. Take care that the removal of older, faster-growing trees does not result in gaps in the windbreak.

Pine is an excellent choice for the middle rows. Although it grows slowly in the first 10 years, it matures to a tall tree with an exceptionally long life. It will be the backbone of the shelterbelt as the whole planting matures. I try to include pine in all of my shelterbelts because it is the most durable of any tree I plant here. Figure 2.6 illustrates the use of Siberian elm for quick protection and evergreens for long term usefulness.

The leeward rows of a shelterbelt are the most protected rows in the whole windbreak. Note the absence of large drifts in this area in Figure 2.5. These trees complete the protection package offered by the shelterbelt, stopping any snow that escaped the windward shrub row and slow-

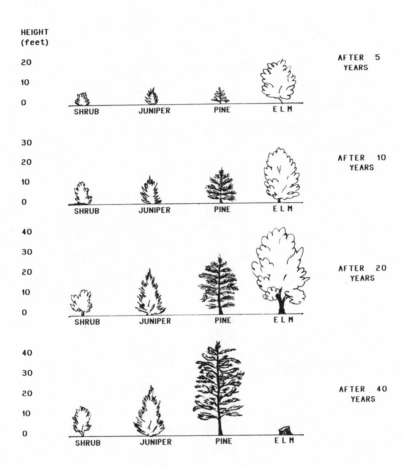

Fig. 2.6. Fast-growing and slow-growing trees and shrubs in a four-row shelterbelt.

ing the wind even more. The leeward row is your last shot at the wind and snow before it hits the object of protection. This row must count.

Cedar and juniper look especially beautiful in the leeward row of a multi-row windbreak. They also provide the greatest density closest to the area being shielded and give an effective brake to the wind and snow. Damage to cedar and juniper from heavy snow is minimized by planting them in this, the most protected row. Granted, the purpose of a shelterbelt is to protect your house or cattle; but the trees also protect each other.

If wildlife is a consideration in your plan, the leeward rows should contain the food-producing shrubs and trees. Animals and birds will be most numerous in these protected rows since the bulk of the snow will remain in the windward rows. Russian olive, buffaloberry, American plum, chokecherry, and honeysuckle provide food for both you and your wildlife friends; at the same time they contribute to the total density of the shelterbelt. Cedar and juniper produce berries as well as wintertime density.

Weeds as Snow Trap

Sometimes information intended for wet regions recommends allowing tall weeds to grow within the tree rows of a shelterbelt to stop snow in winter, but this is a self-defeating practice. The weeds sap more moisture from the trees than they will trap as snow. This method adapted to wetter areas has no place in a dryland setting. Sometimes when the fireweed has gotten ahead of me in late fall and is standing when snow falls, I do pretend that I left it there for snow-stopping purposes. The damage is already done by then; the weeds have already taken whatever moisture they are going to, and they've produced an abundant supply of seeds to replace themselves next year, so I leave them standing to trap snow. I never intend to use this method, though; it only creates more work. I will have to hack out the woody stalks in spring and liberate the trees from the thick carpet of fireweed seedlings that will have sprouted beneath the parent plants. A weed snow fence is cheap, but it is a poor means of trapping snow.

Snow Traps for Individual Trees

Not every tree planting is in a shelterbelt. I have many trees tucked into unused corners or in areas where it is not possible to cultivate a traditional shelterbelt. Sometimes they are in spots where there isn't enough space for a tractor to be operated, on a hillside where cultivation would contribute to erosion, or in a spot too rocky to disk. Trapping snow moisture is equally valuable to these isolated trees. I use my old Christmas tree as a snow-stopper. Laid on its side to the northwest of a tree, it causes a substantial drift to deposit right where the seedling can use it. I also use boughs pruned from orchard trees or evergreens and arrange these in a semi-circle windward from lone trees to serve as a snow trap. On extremely windy sites, it is necessary to stake small boughs to prevent them from tumbling away.

The principle of a snow-trapping shrub row can be applied to a small group of trees as well. I have pine trees growing on the wind-swept hill above our house; snow tends to blow and form a drift over the crest of the hill, out of reach of my pines' roots. I've planted low-growing evergreen shrubs, Pfitzer juniper, to the north of the pine to act as drift-makers. The shrubs are less than 2 feet tall at present, but their thick low branches make an effective snow trap already. They trap moisture not only for the pines, but for themselves as well. Their effectiveness will increase as they grow.

Competition for Moisture

We've seen that weeds compete with your trees for moisture. The trees themselves also vie for moisture against each other. It stands to reason that allowing greater spacing between trees gives them more moisture to draw on. If a tree has the moisture that falls on 40 square feet of land surface, it will grow better than one that has only the moisture from 20 square feet of soil surface.

An important way to ensure that shelterbelt trees have a future is to plant rows far enough apart so that cultivation can continue indefinitely. The prevailing wisdom is that shelterbelts need to be planted with rows so close together that their branches quickly form a solid canopy that will shade out competing weed growth. This works in areas that receive sufficient moisture to support a dense population of trees. In dry regions tree rows need to be farther apart so that each tree has more square footage of soil from which to draw moisture.

Greater spacing between rows accommodates large tillage equipment without damaging low branches on the trees. This is especially important to large-scale operators who may not own small-dimension equipment. Whatever the size of your implements, rows should be at least 4 to 6 feet wider than the equipment. If your disk is 12 feet wide, your row intervals should be no narrower than 16 feet. Greater spacing allows you to cultivate for more years.

Eventually you may have to stop cultivating when tree branches spread across the row, but that day should be postponed as long as possible. Most shelterbelts show little stress in the first years after tillage is ceased, but before long they are completely sodbound and the trees begin to suffer the consequences of having to compete with deep-rooted grass for moisture. Soon the weakest, least hardy trees die out leaving gaps in the windbreak. Although this initially reduces stress for the remaining trees, the shelterbelt as a whole becomes less effective. I'll discuss necessary renovation further in chapter 6.

Our first shelterbelt is a prime example of a planting that will need renovation in the future. Not only is it located on a dry hilltop but the narrowly spaced rows won't allow Bill to cultivate for many more years. We plan to add some well-spaced evergreen rows to the windward side in order to enhance its effectiveness as the other trees decline. We are contemplating removing some of the interior rows so that we can continue cultivation for the rest. This shelterbelt is located in the best spot to provide protection for the buildings, but its dry, hilltop location requires continuous cultivation in order for the trees to survive.

By planting Rocky Mountain juniper, Russian olive, and other drought-resistant species in shelterbelt rows no closer than 16 feet apart, you can cultivate for more years. Less drought-tolerant and larger sized species, such as green ash or honeylocust, need rows spaced as much as 25 feet apart, particularly on unfavorable sites.

Table 2.1 lists suggested minimum space between trees in the row. These recommendations are for areas that get less than 16 inches of moisture. If you are planting in a less-than-ideal location, increase the spacing between rows rather than increase the spacing between individual trees. This way you do not sacrifice snow- and wind-stopping density.

Table 2.1. Minimum row spacing.

Type of Tree or Shrub	Multiple Row Windbreak	Single Row Windbreak
Siberian peashrub Common lilac Tatarian honeysuckle American plum Common chokecherry Silver buffaloberry	5 feet apart	4 feet apart
Russian olive Manchurian apricot	10 feet apart	8 feet apart
Honeylocust Green ash Common hackberry Siberian elm	20 feet apart	10 feet apart
Ponderosa pine	16 feet apart	12 feet apart
Rocky Mountain juniper Eastern red cedar	10 feet apart	8 feet apart

Trees Planted Near Available Water

Plant trees where topography or runoff from buildings increases the availability of water to your trees. Hilltops lose much of the moisture through runoff, so upland soil does not actually benefit from 15 inches of annual precipitation here in our area. Valleys, on the other hand, are the recipients of runoff, so the actual precipitation amount in those areas may be closer to 20 inches.

Taking advantage of existing sources of extra water is an excellent way to give trees an abundance of moisture. For example, I have an elm situated where the gutter delivers water from the barn roof; instead of depending only on the rainfall in the immediate vicinity, the tree receives additional rainfall from an area half the size of the barn. Needless to say, the elm has grown quickly. Likewise, trees that receive runoff from the road or a culvert are much taller than other trees in the same shelterbelt that have only their "own" rainfall and whatever snow they can trap to grow on. Nature does this same thing, growing trees best in valleys and draws. Always be on the lookout for easy water.

I want to plant trees in our summer pasture to provide shade for the cattle. A year ago the sole tree in that pasture died and blew down. I always liked the tree because a pair of bald eagles perched in it whenever they were in the vicinity; they would remain there until 3 P.M. then take off to the east on a hunting foray. I miss the tree because now we only see the eagles if we happen to notice them in flight.

It is no easy task to grow another tree in that pasture; I must look for ways to give it advantages. A draw runs the length of the pasture. During runoff from a January thaw or summer downpour, it fills a stock dam at the lower end. The draw is dry any other time. One spot is watered by a spring, so water remains in a small pond for some time even during a dry spell. Common sense dictates that this spot is excellent for a tree; it will have its own watering system. I have scrounged some used wooden pallets from a building supply store and will fasten these to posts in order to provide protection from cattle and browsing wildlife. I'll plant a hackberry tree because of its ability to withstand tough conditions, its spreading crown, and its berries that are a source of food for birds. It will grow quickly, especially with the spring nearby, but it will be a tree that will endure. I hope the eagles will like it.

The moist area in the draw isn't the only reason that I select this location. The rest of the pasture is relatively flat and nothing taller than native grasses exist there, except for the highline pole that delivers electricity to the well. That pole is struck by lightning every other summer; an isolated tree on the plain would also draw lightning, and cattle seeking shelter under it would take the jolt, too. If we plant trees down in the valley, the cattle will still have shade and the height of the trees will not attract lightning as much.

The flatland of the pasture offers some good places for trees and shrubs, too. Several broad depressions dot the pasture; these collect extra water from rains. I won't plant towering trees here but rather low, spreading trees like Eastern red cedar or Rocky Mountain juniper along with Russian olive or silver buffaloberry. This combination will provide both shelter and a source of food for the sharp-tailed grouse and other wild birds that like our grassland.

Such plantings will need to be fenced in order to protect the trees from damage livestock and wildlife can inflict.

The dam in that pasture is built near rock outcroppings that act as a drain when the dam is full. The little valley below is often quite wet from seepage and would be an excellent place to plant a thicket of food- and shelter-producing trees for wildlife.

With a little careful observation of natural situations, we've found three completely different but excellent spots to put trees, all in one dryland pasture. The trees will need care getting established even in these favored locations, but once they are growing well they will have a good chance of surviving on the moisture collected there. In effect, these sites get more than the 10 to 12 inches of our annual precipitation. Trees growing there get closer to 16 and they're happier with that amount.

We don't irrigate crops on our ranch, but some nearby areas do so using center pivot systems. Sprinklers deliver water to the crop while traveling in a circle around the center of the square field. The corners of the field where the sprinkler doesn't reach may collect additional moisture even though they are not directly irrigated. Trees planted there benefit from the extra water available at the same time they provide protection for the crop.

Summary

The plains aren't a perfect place. Water is in short supply and this limits tree growth. You can't plant a tree on a windy hilltop and expect it to flourish, but the plains boast a few select spots that give a tree an advantage. We always need to be on the lookout for such places. Even when there are no favored sites, we've seen that we can imitate nature and create our own through dead furrows, contouring, soil dams, and basins. We can further increase moisture available to trees by trapping snowfall with snow fences and effective shrub rows in shelterbelts. If one year's supply of moisture is inadequate to establish young trees, we can summerfallow and save up for planting the following year. Trees need a little help to survive and thrive on the plains, and these techniques are just the advantage that helps them succeed.

CHAPTER THREE

Weed Control

Trapping snow and creating water-gathering systems in order to gather soil moisture are only half the job. Preserving that moisture for the tree also means removing the competition from weeds and grasses.

Tree Enemy Number One

Twelve inches of moisture is no great amount, even if the tree gets every drop. And it will get only leftovers surrounded by a healthy crop of weeds. A tree or shrub transplanted from the nursery leaves behind most of its tiny feeder roots and has to spend the first year in the new location regenerating an adequate root system. It is a handicapped plant competing against some of the most adaptive plants in nature. It is not a fair fight by any means.

In a perfect world the trees would grow like weeds, but it's not like that. Turn your back on your tree plantings for a day or two, and you have to beat a lush, 3-foot growth of weeds aside until you find a plant recognizable as a tree. It's down in there, leafed out, but hardly growing in the shade of the greedy weeds.

This will never do; weed control is essential to the survival of trees in a dryland situation. There is no advantage in letting weeds have the water that your trees desperately need. A great variety of methods are useful in weed control, some for cultivated shelterbelt situations and others for individually grown trees.

Cultivation

Cultivation has many purposes in agriculture. We've already discussed its water-conserving value in summer-fallow. Another function of cultivation or tillage in a tree planting is weed control. Whether trees are grown in a shelterbelt or individually, cultivation is used to stir the soil and uproot weeds that steal water from the tree. Sweeps, disks, spring-tooth cultivators, rototillers, and hand-held hoes all do a good job; the one to use depends on the type of tree planting you are cultivating.

Cultivation between Shelterbelt Rows

Use tractor-pulled implements between the rows in shelterbelts. Bill uses a disk that is set to penetrate not more than 4 to 6 inches into the ground in order to avoid injuring small feeder roots close to the soil surface. Frequency of cultivation depends on how much moisture there is, how rapidly more weeds germinate, and how quickly perennial weeds like creeping jenny regrow.

After cultivation, it takes 7 to 10 days for new shoots of jenny to appear, then another 7 to 10 days elapses while the plant uses its root reserves in order to produce new growth. Only after that does the plant begin to build strength and vigor again. Therefore, keeping creeping jenny cultivated at approximately 14- to 20-day intervals will severely weaken it and possibly eliminate it. I'd have to see it eliminated to believe it, but frequent cultivation will certainly suppress it. Similar perennial weeds can be treated the same way.

Cultivation eliminates moisture-robbing weeds very effectively, well enough to make up for the fact that the act of cultivation itself actually causes between 1/4 and 1/2 inch of water to evaporate from the soil. It's far better to lose 1/4 inch of moisture after a good weed-killing cultivation than to lose that amount of water each day from a solid stand of weeds. At the rate of 1/4 inch of moisture per day, weeds use 3-1/2 inches in a 14-day period. I'd rather cultivate every 14 days and use that extra 3-1/2 inches of water to grow trees.

Shelterbelts need to be cultivated between the rows to keep them in optimum condition. If someone from Iowa tells you this is not necessary, he's talking about growing trees in Iowa not on the semiarid plains. Some will advise sowing grass between the rows of trees once they reach a certain height so that the grass can be mowed. What good this would do in a dry area is beyond me. Grass is just as competitive for water as weeds are. If you are growing trees in a climate that does not provide enough moisture for both trees and grass, you have to make a choice. Choose trees.

Cultivation between Trees in a Row

Cultivation takes care of the weeds in the 20 feet

between the tree rows very effectively, but it leaves an 18- to 24-inch strip of weeds growing between and around the trees themselves. The first year it might seem to make more sense to leave the 20 feet weedy and worry only about the 24 inches nearest to trees because that's where the trees' roots are competing with the roots of weeds. You might allow weeds to grow between the rows on a site subject to heavy erosion. In most situations, you cannot forego clean cultivation of the entire shelterbelt, especially between the trees in the row.

A garden rototiller is a good implement to use to cultivate within the tree row. Care must be taken when weaving in and out near the trees to avoid damaging the trunks with the revolving tines. In general a tiller does a good job on small weeds, but cannot chew up stout weeds. Rocky soil may be hard on the machine, so it has limitations. The noise and vibration of the experience may be enough to make you reach for your hoe anyway.

That may not be all bad because a sharp hoe is a foolproof tool for removing weeds. It requires no gasoline or oil changes and can be run by almost anyone. I recommend it. Weeds growing close to the trees still need to be pulled by hand, but this is also true when using a tiller.

Tractor-Mounted, Between-Tree Cultivators

A tree-grower's dream come true is a tractor-mounted implement that cultivates between the trees in the row, eliminating chemicals, mulching, hoeing, and sore backs. Such an amazing machine does exist; some clever individuals have made their own. A commercial model is also on the market. Weed Badger® in Litchville, North Dakota, manufactures an implement that they say gives 99.99 percent perfect weed control and can be adapted to fit any tractor.

Most between-tree cultivators kill weeds with revolving tines that spin weeds from the row; hydraulics move the tool out of the way when a tree approaches. I know of one homemade model mounted on a skid-steer loader that darts in and out between the trees. Some devices can be manually operated to avoid trees; commercial models employ sophisticated sensing equipment so tree damage is avoided. Such cultivators are aggressive enough to chew up sod and the depth of cultivation can be varied.

People who have used these machines are pleased with their performance. The machines do eliminate hand labor and are fast-working once the operator is experienced at maintaining a uniform tractor speed. Although extensions are available to allow use with larger trees, they are best used around trees under five years of age. Their main drawback is the possible damage to trees because of careless operation. They are capable of completely ripping out a 1-inch diameter tree, roots and all.

Cost of the commercial model may be a drawback to many, although the investment may be recouped by doing custom tree cultivation. A custom tree care business would have potential in many areas. People who neither are able nor have time to nurture trees may have money to pay someone else to do the work. A machine would enable one person to completely cultivate many shelterbelts with little or no hand labor, and the owners of the trees would be pleased with the resulting growth. Such a business would net extra income for the operator and would provide a valuable service to the community. Conservation districts sometimes have a machine with an operator available for rent, and often the district has funds to help defray the cost.

Chemical Weed Control

Weed-killing chemicals used among trees come in various forms and are designed to eliminate specifically all broadleaf weeds, such as creeping jenny; only narrow-leaved ones, like grasses; or everything they touch. These chemicals are used to kill weeds that are already growing and are effective on both annual and perennial weeds. Most of these are some variation of 2,4-D and will kill your trees as well as the weeds if the spray contacts foliage or bark.

Preemergence weed-killers prevent weed seeds from germinating and maturing. They are applied to bare soil before weed growth starts. They are available either in the form of granules or spray and must be carried into the upper soil layers by rainfall in order to form a shield which kills germinating seeds. Soil moisture is required for good results; therefore, in dry areas autumn application increases the likelihood that at least some moisture carries the herbicide into the soil. Shallow cultivation also incorporates the material into the top 2 inches of soil. Once the herbicide is in place, the soil surface must not be disturbed. Preemergence herbicides have no effect on perennial plants already in existence, however, and these often flourish even more with less competition from annual weeds.

Herbicide Pros and Cons

Using chemicals to control weeds is feasible but not necessary. It is too easy to damage the trees you are trying to grow. Spray can drift onto tree foliage, and the dying weeds give off volatile chemical residues that affect trees as if they'd been sprayed directly. Applying the spray is not a pleasant task because the stuff smells bad and probably is bad. The spray must be applied when there is no wind, which tends to delay the job. Meanwhile the weeds are sapping 1/4 inch of water every breezy day. Cultivation or weed pulling can be done despite the wind.

Herbicides are not perfectly effective. Bindweed, for instance, can develop resistance to 2,4-D so that the herbicide wipes out the susceptible plants and leaves the tough ones. On the other hand, no one has ever heard of a weed becoming resistant to a rototiller. Herbicides are most effective on a vigorously growing plant. In a drought, when the weeds are hanging on but not growing rampantly, spraying is not going to harm them much. They will continue to compete with your trees for what little moisture is left.

Preemergence herbicides cannot be applied until the fall of the first tree-growing season because young seedlings react to the chemical the same way that the germinating seeds do; they die. Contact herbicides that kill weeds already up and growing may still be used around young trees, however.

Chemical weed control tends to be less labor-intensive in subsequent years, and may allow one person to care for more trees than controlling weeds solely by tractor or hand cultivation. Keeping a large shelterbelt weed-free may become too burdensome without the use of herbicides, and their careful use may be justified.

Caution with Herbicides

Herbicides can be dangerous. Extreme care needs to

be taken in selecting, mixing, and applying herbicides. The advice of a competent chemical expert or extension service person should be sought and followed to the letter.

Above all, avoid getting herbicide on the foliage of your trees. Use a low-pressure spray with large droplets, since these drift less in the wind. Spray only on calm days. Even a light wind can cause the herbicide to contact your trees. Physically protecting the tree is the best way to avoid herbicide damage. A 2-foot section of stove pipe set over small trees effectively prevents the spray from contacting the foliage. For larger trees, a 5-gallon pail with its bottom cut out does the same job. A light-weight board or piece of paneling placed between the tree and spray is also effective. Plastic, commercially available tree shelters employed to enhance growth and protect against animal damage are also effective in preventing spray damage.

These tactics will prevent spray from actually getting on the needles and leaves of your trees. However, nearby weeds that get sprayed can emit gases lethal to your trees, particularly with certain types of herbicide formulations. Spraying when the air temperature is above 90°F makes the herbicide especially volatile and deadly.

Use the smallest amount of herbicide that you can. Time your applications so that they will do the most good. Spray when the weeds are almost ready to bloom because they are most vulnerable at this point. A spray application in fall while the plants are still growing weakens them for winter.

Different soil types require different rates of application for some chemicals, especially preemergents. Further, it is necessary to calibrate the amount of spray you are applying over the intended area. Chemical weed control is not a matter of simply mixing up powder in a can and going out to spray weeds. If you are not extremely careful, you can damage yourself, your trees, and the environment. Weigh all of this carefully before you proceed.

If you are determined that you cannot grow trees without herbicides, but do not have the expertise or equipment to do a good job, consider hiring a chemical firm to do it for you. Many businesses handling agricultural chemicals also do custom work. They will know how to apply herbicides correctly. You are still responsible for knowing and evaluating the chemicals these companies use, however. It is your water and soil that may be polluted by poor use of herbicides, so it is your job to prevent that from happening.

Accidental Herbicide Spray Drift

The accidental application of herbicides can also be devastating to trees. Field windbreaks are especially subject to damage by the chemicals that are used to control weeds in the adjoining cropland. A tree is a broadleaf plant and reacts the same as creeping jenny does to a broadleaf herbicide. A single dose of herbicide doesn't always kill the entire tree, but large portions of its canopy can be damaged. Repeated exposure is usually fatal.

When Bill was growing up on a ranch east of the Black Hills, he and his family worked hard growing a beautiful five-row shelterbelt near their ranch buildings. It provided protection to both cattle and crops and was an eye-catcher on the flat prairie. When the place was sold, however, the new owners apparently didn't appreciate the trees very much. Spray drift badly damaged the entire shelterbelt.

Ten years of work was wiped out with just a few careless passes of a spray plane.

Mulch

Cultivation by machine or hand is definitely the method of choice for shelterbelt trees, but not all trees are planted in neat rows. For instance, I have pine and cedar trees planted behind our house. The area is too small, too sloping, and too rock-infested for a tractor to maneuver. If tractor cultivation were the only way possible to control weeds and grass in that situation, no trees would be growing there, or they would be growing poorly. For plantings such as this, mulch is very effective in eliminating weed competition and at the same time, preventing excess evaporation of soil moisture.

Mulching is merely copying nature; the leaf litter under forest trees is nature's recycling program in action. When we first planted the pine trees behind our house, we watered them faithfully, but they grew only a few inches every year while the ones left untransplanted in my father's timberland were twice as tall. Of course, the shock of transplanting, difference in soil, and the loss of root area needs to be considered. The big difference, however, was that grass grew right up to the trunks on my trees; in my father's woods a thick layer of pine needles kept the grass thinned out. Nature had perfected this plan, but it took me a while to catch on. I had used mulch in my garden to advantage, and it soon proved to work just as well on my trees.

Mulch has the advantage of being able to be put exactly where the tree needs the most protection from weed competition. The tree's meager roots are struggling in an area roughly equal to the spread of its canopy, so the circle of mulch can start relatively small and grow as the tree grows.

One of the best features of a mulched tree is that the work can be done in the slack season; often I take advantage of warm days in late winter to mulch my trees. When spring and summer come, I can tend to other trees while my mulched ones are nestled safe from drought and weeds. Depending on the type of mulch employed, once the mulch is laid it is sufficient for at least a season. Mulching is a recycler's dream; most mulch materials are ones that can't be used anywhere else and are either headed for the dump or already there.

Admittedly, mulches of all kinds will keep light rains from reaching the soil where a tree could use it. Some people use this as an argument against mulching, but I don't think this is a grave enough concern to avoid use of this valuable tree-growing method. Often 1/4 inch of rain evaporates before noon the next day, even on bare soil. This doesn't help the tree. Rain seeping into a mulch may fare better because the mulch protects what rain it gets. Cultivation also is responsible for loss of moisture every time the soil is stirred and exposed to drying wind. Furthermore, cultivation adds no humus and nutrients to the soil. An organic mulch that decays and adds humus to the soil will give the soil greater ability to absorb water in a major rain. This will help make up for the light rains that never reach tree roots. Mulch has the ability to curtail growth of moisture-robbing weeds and protect soil from hot, drying winds. This more than compensates for the small amount of moisture it keeps out. Mulch used atop a drip system is ideal because barely a molecule of added water is lost.

To lessen the chance of mulch keeping rain water away from the soil, I make sure that I have provided a catchment basin, or saucer. With the tree at the lowest point in its center, and mulch applied over the soil, rainfall is directed to where the tree needs it most. (See Figure 3.1.)

The type of material you choose to use for mulch on your trees is limited only by your imagination and by what you can scrounge up. If you live near a sawmill, use sawdust, bark or wood chips. If you live near a sugar beet processing plant, use beet by-products. For example, I don't mulch with corn cobs because they aren't available here, but I admire them every time we travel in corn country. Someday I'm going to haul a load home and see how they work.

I like to use things that eventually will disintegrate because they will improve the soil's ability to hold water, and will not create a minidump under my trees. I don't like to use plastic for a mulch because eventually it shreds and blows around the ranch unless it's weighted. Fences festooned with ribbons of plastic are not my idea of beauty.

Fig. 3.1. Mulched tree planted in a basin.

But who needs plastic? There are wood chips, saw-dust, straw, old hay, used livestock bedding, junk mail, magazines, newspapers, grass clippings, bark, rocks and my favorite—old carpet.

Wood Chips

Wood chips are available in our area from a company that sends chipped pine to Wisconsin for making paper. They usually have a large pile mixed with dirt that can't be used for paper, and are willing to load it for me. The small shredders designed to make mulch out of garden waste and pruned limbs also produce usable chips.

Wood chips look good and don't decompose for several years. I like that feature because a tree is taken care of for quite some time, and I don't need to repeat the mulching job every year. We have mulched our orchard with wood chips, in combination with a drip irrigation system. It seems to be working well even during drought years. A few weeds peek through, but these can be pulled as if they're rooted in pudding. The soil is soft and mellow beneath the chips; earthworms abound in the moist ground. Of all the mulch materials I've used, I believe wood chips allow the most rainfall to enter the soil and do the best job retaining that moisture.

Before we put down the chips, we had mulched with wasted hay and manure from around the stationary hay feeder in the corral. This gave the soil a boost in nitrogen to help the microorganisms break down the carbon-rich wood chips. Wood chips are very poor in nitrogen but need nitrogen in order to break its fiber into humus. Since the chips are used for mulch and not incorporated into the soil, little of their volume is decayed in any year. It would not be a good idea to disk them into the soil because you would create a temporary nitrogen shortage for your plants. The same is true of any organic material that is high in carbon, such as sawdust, pine needles, or even paper. You will cause no such shortage by using these for mulch on top of the soil. For this reason, mulch is best used on individually grown trees that are not ordinarily cultivated. If you try to mulch around cultivated shelterbelt trees, tillage will incorporate the mulch into the soil and cause a nitrogen shortage.

I have seen no harm come to plants or trees if pine sawdust or chips are used only as a mulch. Some say that a toxin in these materials causes plants to yellow and die, but this is the nitrogen shortage that I described. Do not incorporate them into the soil before decay takes place. Cedar and black walnut residues are known to be toxic to plants, and should not be used for mulch. Also they aren't available in quantity. Chips and sawdust from hardwoods should be composted for 30 to 60 days to remove toxic substances, but softwood chips may be used immediately.

Magazines and Newspapers

Usually magazines, newspapers, and junk mail are more readily available than most mulch materials. Newspaper printing companies sometimes have foot-thick bundles of newspapers to get rid of. Junk mail comes to our house in such quantities that I've threatened to install a barrel next to the mailbox for direct deposit, no matter how many millions they rave about in the sweepstakes mailings. This is one alternative. Mulching is another.

Magazines and newspapers with colored ink are harmful because the ink contains toxins you wouldn't want to eat. I never use colored ink materials in my garden, orchard, or around food-producing shrubs. None of my livestock has access to my tree-plantings under any circumstances, so they are not at risk either.

While there is some chance of releasing harmful toxins into the environment from colored inks, this danger also exists if you send them to a landfill. At least if I use magazines to mulch a nonfood-producing tree, they will have a balancing positive effect in the form of a magnificent tree.

Magazines last two to four years beneath another layer of mulch, giving a good start to a tree. Rainfall and oxygen can still pass through to the roots, yet most annual weeds cannot make all the right twists and turns necessary to grow up through the overlapped layers. Perennial weeds are apt to regard the paper barrier as a mere setback. Newspapers don't last as long as dense magazines, but they make a good solid barrier. The major drawback to using paper is that you can't work with it on a very windy day because it blows away easily. Dipping it first in a bucket of water helps make it too soggy for the wind to take. Of course, paper mulches must be anchored by a heavier mulch over the top to keep them from blowing away. Their main purpose is reducing the depth needed for the upper mulch because the paper is so efficient in keeping out weeds.

Tree Bark

I like bark as a mulch because it is nice-looking and I can get it. We cut pine trees and peel them for posts. The peeler strips the bark off in shreds and shoots them in a high arc into a pile. I haul this pile home. Another source of bark, in small quantities, is that which falls off the firewood into the bottom of the wood box.

Pine Needles

Similarly, I can get pine needles if I keep my eyes open. One year members of our church helped rake pine needles from a chapel lawn in the city. Naturally, I volunteered to take the pine needles. Bill drove home with a 20-foot stock trailer packed to the ceiling with needles. For days after, I felt like a wealthy woman scurrying around lavishly mulching my trees.

Sawdust

Sawdust's availability varies according to other uses the sawmill owner has for it. Sometimes it is used to fuel kilns or is bagged for sale as bedding. If you ask often enough and are in the right place at the right time, you'll come across some sawdust free for the hauling.

Sawdust does have a drawback: its fine particles tend to blow away in 50-mph wind gusts. On the exposed hill behind our house I've had to protect the sawdust with pine boughs. The pines near the east line fence are protected by a row of elms, and the sawdust doesn't blow away there. On balance, though, it's a very satisfactory mulch. It's easy to work with. A scoopful is not heavy; it smells great; it's dense enough to discourage weeds well with only a 4- to 5-inch layer, and it lasts a long time.

Grass Clippings

Grass clippings work well as tree mulch, but I usually use these only in my garden. I need the extra fertility the clippings give the soil there. Their rapid rate of decay serves the garden well; a tree would be crying for more before the summer was out. I generally don't have enough clippings to use on trees; but if you do, they make excellent mulch. They have a high nitrogen-to-carbon ratio so they break down easily and enrich the soil. Earthworms riddle the soil beneath a grass clipping mulch in their haste to pull it deeper into the earth. Just make sure that no herbicides have been applied to the lawn before it was mowed and the clippings collected. Residues on the clippings can be detrimental to your garden and trees.

Leaves

Deciduous tree leaves make a good mulch, rotting in the course of a year or two and providing humus to the soil. They have drawbacks, though. Whole leaves blow easily; if you're not careful, you'll rake them twice. Either use them in an area protected from wind (this leaves out much of the plains), shred them with a lawn mower to make the pieces too small and matted to be caught by the wind, or cover them with a heavier layer, such as straw.

Leaves are no problem to acquire; they are found beneath any deciduous tree in fall. Rake your own, or let your friends know that you are taking all the leaves you can get your hands on. If you're lucky, the leaves will come to you already bagged. Don't neglect nearby cities as a source of leaves, too.

Rocks

Lacking a supply of organic materials to work with, it is practical to use rocks. Nature does. Rocks are usually all too available, especially when you are mowing a hayfield. I pile the rocks around the tree atop a layer of newspapers. Even when the paper eventually rots, the rocks will protect the moisture in the soil from evaporation in the hot sun and strong wind. Large flat rocks are ideal since they provide more continuous cover. Small rocks work well if they are more than one layer deep. Do not nestle the rocks so closely around the trunk that the bark will be abraded by the edges of the rocks when the wind whips the sapling. It's a good idea to make sure that the tree you're rock mulching is growing well before you mulch it. It is difficult to replace a tree that's surrounded by 500 pounds of rocks.

Even creeping jenny can't penetrate a rock. The stones at least cut down on the weed growth in later years after the paper is gone. By then, the tree should be better established and able to compete for moisture; the rocks will give it the edge on survival. Happily, mulching with rocks is a job that never needs to be repeated. Rocks don't rot.

Stone mulching accomplishes all these tasks at once: I get the coffee table cleaned off when I'm collecting magazines, the tree gets mulched, and the hayfields are in better shape when I finish picking out rocks. Furthermore, we save the wear and tear on the machinery that stones cause.

I used a stone mulch on a row of Siberian elm in the shelterbelt by the well. We had planted the elms on the very edge of the shelterbelt with the idea that they would grow quickly and provide protection for the cattle until the slower-growing, but permanent, planting of ponderosa pine and Rocky Mountain juniper was large enough to do the job. We could remove the entire elm row if they started to interfere with cultivation of the pines. Since they were planted on the edge of the shelterbelt, we could cultivate on only one side; the other edge was dense grass. I had put a temporary mulch over the grass, but the stone mulch that replaced it will last even longer than the trees.

A row of lilacs grows next to the fence in our yard. On the yard side, I had used straw to mulch a 4-foot strip to keep the grass from competing with the bushes, but the slope on the other side of the fence was thick with fireweed. It looked terrible from the road, and every time I watered the lilacs I was watering the fireweed as well. Now that's all changed; we hauled large flat rocks and fitted them together from the fence to the bottom of the slope. We plan to cement them in to prevent slippage and to keep weeds from growing between the rocks. This may not take place right away, so I laid magazines beneath the rocks to keep the weeds at bay until we can do the cement job. The rocks improved the looks of the area, but they're actually there to help my lilacs grow.

Plastic Mulch

For me, plastic mulch is a mulch of last resort. It contributes nothing to the soil under any circumstances, no matter how long it lasts. Water can't soak through, and it deprives the roots of oxygen. Its dark color absorbs heat from the sun and bakes the soil and roots beneath. I use it rarely. I did use it on some pine trees that I transplanted from my father's land into a furrow that Bill plowed for me in an otherwise wasted corner of a shelterbelt. I covered the furrow and several feet on either side with black plastic. Slits in the plastic allowed the trees to poke through and let the buckets of water that I poured in soak down to the soil; some rain water will drain off into the holes as well. Knowing that the plastic would billow and blow like a circus tent on a windy day, I covered it with oat straw, anchoring the edges with stones and sod clods. In addition to keeping the plastic from flopping, the straw kept the black color of the plastic from heating the soil and air surrounding my little trees. I provided shade and protection from south winds for the trees, and lost only one out of ten pine trees—not bad in a year that set records for heat and drought.

Recent improvements of black plastic have eliminated many of the drawbacks. New "filter fabrics" are made of heavy duty polypropylene that won't easily disintegrate. They stop weeds from growing because they are opaque to sunlight, yet they have the ability to allow air, water, and nutrients to pass through to the soil. Some brands must be covered with another mulch to prevent the sunlight from breaking down or disintegrating the plastic. This is a disadvantage; but near your home, you'll probably want the fabric covered with a more natural-looking mulch anyway. Types of fabric that stand exposure to the sun are being used between the trees in shelterbelt rows. This eliminates all chemical and hand weed control other than cultivation between rows. Cost of the plastic fabric is the principle drawback in using it on an entire shelterbelt, but cost-sharing may be available from government conservation agencies.

Plastic Irrigation Pipe

Irrigators often use plastic pipe these days. It is a long tube of plastic of about the same gauge as the black stuff normally used for mulch. It lasts only one season as irrigation pipe and then is rolled back up on the huge spool that it came on and is discarded. When slit the entire length, it folds out to a 2-foot width, a usable size for mulching. It is free, but as a mulch it doesn't last much longer than it does as irrigation pipe. Worse yet, it disintegrates into little shreds and is a nuisance to clean up. If it's covered with soil or straw, it lasts longer because the sun can't degrade it. If there were no other mulch available, however, using plastic irrigation pipe would be better than letting the trees die, which is why I mention this mulch source.

Plastic mulch must be popular with someone because 285 million pounds of petroleum-based plastic film are produced each year for agricultural use alone; half of that is used for mulch. It needs to be disposed of at the end of its usefulness; just what happens to it in a dump is something that archaeologists 500 years from now may discover. A new type of mulching film that decomposes naturally is being developed from surplus corn.

Carpet

Plastic doesn't allow any weed to grow through it, but I've talked about its disadvantages. There is one kind of mulch that does not allow weed growth yet has none of the disadvantages of plastic: used, jute-backed carpet. Don't use foam-backed carpet because it acts as a sponge over the soil instead of letting rain sink in. Also the foam material tends to slough off and be a trash and environmental problem. Some carpet has a plastic coating on the back that repels rainwater; avoid this type completely. One piece of carpet that was given me smelled strongly of ammonia used in cleaning it. I did not use this piece in mulching because my tree probably couldn't have stood the smell of ammonia any better than I could.

Hot pink shag, nondescript gray from the halls of a drab office, grass-green plush. Turn it all upside-down and it's a soft shade of brown that blends in with any soil, tree, or shrub. No matter how verdant the weeds beneath a newly planted tree, a square of old carpet fitted snugly around the tree allows only the tree to grow on the moisture there. Rain seeps through, oxygen gets into the soil, and evaporation is practically eliminated.

Carpeting my trees has become my mulching method of choice. It looks neat, and it is the most effective mulch I've found. Using carpet for mulch makes use of something that would otherwise burden an already overflowing land-fill, and it costs me nothing but the hauling. Sometimes hauling is not required; I have contacted the local garbage disposal company and they save for me the carpet that their customers are throwing out. Instead of paying to deposit it in the dump, they haul it to me.

Heavy wire bent into the shape of a 6-inch staple and pushed into the earth through the carpet edges anchors it. The staples also keep the carpet from catching in the lawn mower; you can mow over it and keep a neat-looking border around the mulched tree. Mowing around other mulches tends to be a problem because the mower blade sucks up chips or straw and distributes them elsewhere. Once you put the carpet down, that's where it stays. Chickens can't even scratch it out.

It isn't difficult to work with carpet; although the rolls can be heavy until they're cut. A utility knife works well to slice carpet provided a new blade is installed from time to time. Cut on the back side of the carpet; it's easier, and the weave of the backing helps guide your knife.

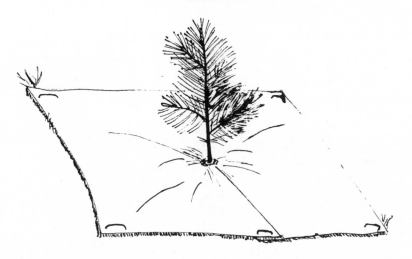

Fig. 3.2. Anchored carpet mulch.

Before you install old carpet around the tree, dig a shallow saucer for water collection first. This is essential. Slope the saucer downward toward the trunk of the tree so that when the carpet is laid around the tree, rainfall will drain toward the center and water the tree more effectively. To install the carpet, slice from the middle of the piece, where the tree will stick out, to the outer edge. The carpet then can be fitted around the tree with no damage to trunk or branches and anchored with makeshift staples. I leave a little extra space around the tree to give it room to grow without abrasion by the carpet backing. Figure 3.2 shows a carpeted tree.

When you lay the carpet in the saucer around your tree, shape the piece into an inverted cone by overlapping the cut ends several inches. Secure the ends with staples so that weeds won't be tempted to make a break for the light between them. Both the cone shape and the overlapping are vital to the success of this method. The cone funnels what rainfall can't soak through the carpet quickly enough into the center of the growing space.

The size of the carpeted area around a tree depends mostly on how much carpet I have, how many trees I need to mulch, and what the surrounding vegetation is like. If I put a 3-foot diameter piece of carpet around a tree that's planted amid 4-foot-tall brome grass, the grass stems lop over the tree as if the carpet wasn't there. A larger piece keeps both the grass roots and stems at bay. If I am short of carpet, I cover only a 3-foot square area and plan to increase it later. If I have plenty, I lay an 8-foot chunk out and put the tree in the middle. A circle of carpet looks nice surrounding a tree and is easier to mow, but squares are less wasteful and more efficient to cut.

If I encounter holes cut out of the carpet, I lay another chunk of carpet beneath. The bottom piece must be large enough to provide overlap, so that weeds won't find the breach. If I'm using carpet in smaller sections, I try to plan around holes, but if I'm laying large areas, I use this patching method.

I've used carpet for mulch for six years, and some of my original carpet is still in use. It is faded and softer than when I put it down. In a few places, it has started to rot and simply disappear into the soil. Creeping jenny has unerringly found the rotted areas, but if the tree is sufficiently established I do nothing. If I feel that the tree needs additional time free of competition, I recarpet it. I haven't had any problems with disposal yet, but it is possible that some of my carpet will require a trip to the dump.

Carpet is one of the easiest mulches to work with. Once a carpet mulching is complete, it is finished for several years. It does not need to be renewed periodically like straw or other quickly degrading mulch, allowing me time to grow more trees. For these reasons, I use carpet in a variety of tree-growing situations.

Teaming Mulch Materials

Often my mulching methods combine several materials. Usually my isolated trees are planted in grass sod that needs to be eradicated if my trees are to grow. Most of the time a water-collecting saucer is required and the grass is eliminated when I dig the saucer. But sometimes I plant in a low spot and don't wish to lower the planting site farther. In these situations, it's tough to kill a perennial weed with traditional mulch; the shoots simply push up through the straw or wood chips and grow better than ever because they like mulch, too. Grass is no exception. I needed some method to kill the grass, while at the same time preserving moisture for my trees. Overlapping layers of newspapers, junk mail, and magazines proved to be the answer because they totally obliterate sunlight to the soil. (See Figure 3.3.) The grass stems and roots die and rot, eventually releasing plant nutrients to the lucky trees. Another tier of mulch, such as wood chips or straw, is absolutely essential. It covers the paper layer negating any problems with appearance. The layer of chips or straw also keeps the papers from taking off in the first big wind.

Such a treatment will give the tree good growing conditions for several seasons, maybe more if I've used a thick layer of slow-rotting mulch over the paper. The mulch prevents summer winds from reaching the soil and depleting moisture before the tree can use it. It also keeps annual

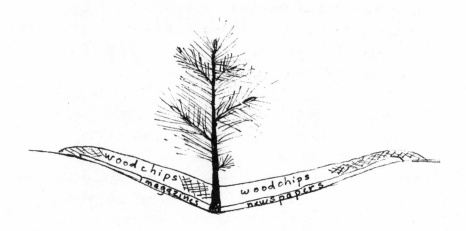

Fig. 3.3. Teaming mulch materials.

weeds from germinating and competing for nutrients and moisture. The mulch itself eventually rots into humus, which increases the soil's ability to hold water.

Carpet mulch can be combined with other tree-growing materials and methods. It is ideal used with drip irrigation. For instance, in the pine row of the shelterbelt by our well, I have installed a drip pipe to help get the trees established. The plastic pipe lies beneath the carpet, so none of the irrigation water is wasted or even meets the sunshine. The carpet helps keep the ultraviolet light of the sun from degrading the plastic pipe.

Mulch Is Attractive

To look at my trees, you'd never know that they were kept alive by junk mail. A healthy tree surrounded by a circle of clean wood chips is all that a casual observer would see. Tree bark or sawdust are equally attractive. My spruce trees are mulched 6 inches deep with pine needles and an occasional cone here and there. The soft brown of the needles sets off the spruce trees beautifully. In any event, they won't be seen much longer as the boughs grow to meet between the trees.

If I do have unattractive mulch, such as livestock bedding, I use it on trees that aren't in the front yard. Bedding rich with manure tends to have a pungent odor, but even that rots down to a mellow pile in a few months and is not offensive. Also it's better for the tree than sawdust because it enriches the soil at a more rapid rate.

Thickness of Mulch Layer

A 5-inch layer of wood chips is wonderful for keeping out weeds, but a mulch of sawdust need not be that thick. Its particles are smaller and more densely packed, allowing less light to reach germinating weed seeds. A large-particle material, such as oat or wheat straw, would need to be much deeper because it is not very dense. Putting a layer of magazines down first will decrease the thickness of the wood chip or straw mulch needed because the paper shuts out light to the weeds.

Mulch for Shelterbelt Trees

Mulch is an effective way both to decrease weed growth and conserve moisture. Most organic mulch methods are not practical for use between trees in the rows in shelterbelts, however. If mulch, such as wood chips, is spread between the trees, cultivation of the rows disturbs the edges of the mulch and incorporates it into the soil. This destroys its efficiency in weed control and may cause problems with nitrogen deficiency.

Other than the new plastic fabrics being experimented with, the only effective mulch material that I've found for use in shelterbelt settings is carpet. I cut old carpet into chunks that are the width of the uncultivated strip between the rows, usually 15-inch pieces, and fit them around the trees as soon as they are planted. If I have an abundance of carpet, I cover the entire row; but this takes a lot of carpet.

Carpeting around each tree is even valuable in keeping the weeds away from the immediate root zone of the young trees. The area between the rows can still be cultivated as usual. Bill occasionally hooks a carpet chunk with the disk, especially if one piece is larger than the rest or if my tree row is crooked.

If you feel that herbicides are essential to your tree-growing success, carpet can be a tool to help keep the spray away from your trees. No weeds grow in the carpeted area close to the trees. No spray will be necessary there, resulting in less chance of accidental herbicide damage. The best part is that the carpet will reduce the need for herbicides in the first place.

Cultivation versus Mulch

Neither cultivation nor mulch is a perfect method. Creeping jenny wiggles through any mulch except carpet or plastic, mulches decay and must be replaced with materials that may be in short supply. Cultivation, on the other hand, must be repeated regularly during the growing season. Unlike mulch, it cannot be completed at less busy times of the year. The equipment required to till the soil makes it more expensive than mulching. Tillage can be responsible for soil erosion while mulch prevents erosion.

I grow trees with both methods, so I have been able to compare the results of each. My test plots are inexact and my results vary. I have had satisfactory tree growth with both techniques as long as both are well performed. Comparing an inadequate mulch job to meticulous cultivation is like comparing apples and oranges. Where my mulched areas are large enough—6 to 8 feet in diameter around a tree—growth has been comparable to trees grown using cultivation to control weeds and grasses.

Because materials are limited, the mulched area is often smaller; but a cultivated tree has a minimum area the width of the disk on all sides. In this situation, there is no question but that the cultivated tree will exceed the growth of the inadequately mulched one. My cultivated plantings are usually in more favorable locations than the rocky hillsides and spare corners I reserve for mulched trees, so it is difficult to make accurate judgments.

Perhaps it is most significant that I have no comparisons between trees grown with one or the other of these methods and trees completely unmulched or uncultivated. Those in the latter group are all dead. Both mulching and cultivating succeed in growing trees.

Summary

The methods described in this chapter require a great deal of effort, yet they are not optional on a dryland site on the plains. They are the extra help a tree needs in order to survive. If weed control is performed with diligence, trees grow more rapidly, and, equally important, the need to supplement natural precipitation with irrigation water is lessened.

CHAPTER FOUR

Boosting Tree Survival Rate

Twelve inches of precipitation is scarcely enough to keep tough, mature trees alive, and definitely not enough for tiny seedlings. Remember that the immature and handicapped root system under those little twigs you plant do not yet have the means to reach out for the water. You may have to bring it to them if rainfall and soil storage from snowfall aren't enough. Even with the water-trapping and conserving measures just discussed, moisture in many years will be short, and you need to be prepared to water your trees during drought years.

Watering seedings in the first growing season helps establish trees and stimulate growth. After the first year or two if they can't survive on their own aided by mulch or cultivation, they are the wrong kinds of trees to plant in a semiarid location. The wise use of limited water supplies begins by planting trees and shrubs that naturally require little water. It's extremely frivolous to plant a weeping willow requiring irrigation to ensure its survival on an upland prairie. Plant a tough species and apply water wisely.

The most important time to water is immediately after planting; this watering should not be ignored no matter how tired you are from planting 500 trees. A soaking right after planting helps settle the soil around the roots so they do not dry out and die—it's a good idea even in fairly moist soil. I generally provide a little saucer around my shelterbelt trees, and a big saucer around my mulched individual trees, so that a basin is ready when I arrive with the water.

I water all my trees in their first year and keep an eye on moisture conditions in subsequent years. If they are having a tough time, I may water even three-year-old trees. Evergreens are more difficult to establish; a steady supply of water is important to their survival. My evergreens get watered for at least two years, and sometimes more if they aren't doing as well as I'd like. It is difficult to predict how much water a tree is going to require in an erratic climate such as ours, so you may end up watering trees once a week, or perhaps as infrequently as once a summer if rains come regularly.

Watering during the second and third years is usually optional if weed competition is kept to a minimum. By this time, the trees should have root systems developed well enough to search out moisture, especially if they aren't in a life-and-death struggle with weeds.

The advantage of watering during the second and third years is that the trees grow much faster, and they will reach the point of providing wind protection, shade, or snow control that much sooner. You've taken land out of production in order to plant trees; by watering them regularly in the beginning, you are harvesting the benefits a few years earlier. It's a trade-off: water the trees and they'll serve you sooner, or save the water and wait longer to reap the benefits.

Amount of Water and Soil Types

Watering rate recommendations are difficult to specify because of variability in soil types. Soils on the plains vary widely from sandy to dense clay. They differ in their ability to absorb, retain, and release moisture to tree roots. For instance, silt loam may hold 2 1/2 inches of moisture per foot, while sandy soil may store only 1/4 inch. Determining how much to water begins with understanding what type of soil you are dealing with.

A county agent, agriculture teacher, or specialist from a government agriculture agency can help you determine what lies beneath your sod. To conduct a simple soil texture test, pick up a handful of moist, but not soaking wet, soil and squeeze it into a ball. If it falls apart immediately, your soil is sandy. If it forms a tight ball that falls apart when you poke it, you have loam. If the tight ball doesn't crumble, the soil has a high proportion of clay. Sandy soil tends to feel gritty when rubbed between the fingers, clay soil will feel slippery, and loam combines the features of both these types.

Sandy soil does not retain water very well, due to the large spaces between the soil fragments. You'll find that you need to water more frequently for trees grown on sandy soil. Although rainwater is absorbed easily into this type of soil, it also drains below the root systems too quickly.

Clay soil has very little space between its particles; it

is difficult for water as well as air and plant roots to penetrate. It drains poorly and dries out slowly. However, once it has soaked up moisture, it is able to hold the most water of any soil type. This is not to say that clay soils can release that water back to plants. Plants aren't able to use every last drop of water in soil because soil moisture resists the pull exerted by plant roots. Clay soils especially hold their moisture against the force of roots.

Loam is the most desirable soil. Although it cannot store as much water as clay, more water is available to the plants. Loam soils are frequently high in organic matter and will retain and release more water to the plants.

The tree species you grow also determines the amount you will need to water. For instance, green ash needs more water than the extremely drought-tolerant silver buffaloberry. A steady supply of moisture is especially critical to ever-greens, particularly in their first year.

In general, saturate the soil to a depth equal to the height of the tree. In loamy soil, water will usually go down at the same rate as it will spread laterally, unless there is a change in soil type close to the surface. To gauge the behavior of water in particular soils, use a small auger or probe to determine the depth of saturation.

Frequency of watering depends on soil type, natural rainfall, tree species, temperature, wind, and the amount of conserved moisture. For instance, a pine tree planted in sandy soil during a hot, dry, and windy spell in mid-summer requires more frequent irrigation than a silver buffaloberry grown in heavy, well-mulched soil during a period of cool weather.

During the first year, waterings should be as frequent as twice a week if the weather is dry. In their first season, trees need approximately one gallon of water per week. This is about the amount a tree would receive over the 3-foot square area around its roots from one inch of rainfall. The second year they need 2 gallons per week, applied at the rate of 4 to 5 gallons every second week in order to encourage the roots to be more aggressive and to spread deeper and fan out farther in the soil. The third year, 15 gallons every third week is sufficient. Hopefully, rain will account for much of this amount; these figures are given as a suggested minimum. You'll be able to tell how much water is needed by simply looking at your trees. If they show stress from lack of water, such as wilting, stunted leaves, or poor growth, you need to water more.

If you water young trees all summer, they keep putting out eager growth heedless of preparing for winter. Gradually stop watering about three weeks before frost is expected. This cues your seedlings to prepare for the end of their growing season. Hardening-off is a set of physiological changes that prepare the plants for survival in the winter. All trees should go into winter with moist soil, but evergreens especially need a few more drinks after frost because they still transpire in winter. They should go into the winter with good moisture reserves or they suffer drought during the winter. Frozen soil won't absorb water, so watering should be done in early autumn.

Watering Methods

It's not easy to water your trees when the water source is a half mile away. Many trees got their start with a bucket of water dipped from a barrel on the back of a pickup. There's nothing wrong with that method except that it takes a lot of time and requires heavy lifting.

Tanks and Barrels

Water trees with whatever you have on hand. If a barrel is all you've got, use a barrel, but keep your eyes open for other possibilities. People around here often arrive at prairie fires with water tanks as large as entire pickup boxes, some equipped with pumps. A tree grower's dream come true is that they hold enough water to do an entire shelterbelt row. A single person can water trees this way. Two make the job go more smoothly because one drives the pickup and the other is the water boss.

For watering trees that are far from the water source, I use a 55-gallon barrel equipped with a shut-off valve on the end of a hose. I place it in the cargo bed of a five-wheel, all terrain vehicle. I must hop on and off frequently, but I can get close enough to the trees to do a good job.

Drip Irrigation

I prefer drip irrigation where feasible because the system is always ready to go. I can attend to other jobs while my trees are being watered one drip at a time. The system applies water only to the root zone and at rates which allow water to soak deeply into the soil. Less water is needed because none is wasted through evaporation, collected in ditches as runoff, or sloshed out of the barrel.

When a water source is nearby, drip systems make watering trees so easy that you water them more often. I try to get my system in place and ready to go before I even plant the trees. I can irrigate right after planting and won't get so busy with something else that I neglect them. When I install a drip system before the trees are planted, I mark the emitter holes with a squirt of spray paint to the upper side of the pipe so I know where to plant the tree. It's handy to mark them anyway so you don't have to search for the holes if they become plugged. However, if you are planning to use a tractor-pulled tree planter, the drip system will have to be installed immediately after planting.

Assembling Your Own System: My drip systems are simple, but they deliver the water where I want it and for much less than one dollar per tree. I am not mechanically inclined, but I can put together my own drip systems with materials from a hardware store.

Most of my systems are 300 feet or less in length and usually laid out in a straight line. Water pressure will vary from my well to yours, so the number of trees that can be watered from any given line footage will also vary. I determine this through trial and error: I lay out my line, turn the water on, and start drilling holes. I determine how many holes I can punch by the amount of water squirting out of each successive hole I install. If the amount of water coming out of the last hole I drill is more than sufficient to water that tree, I know that another hole farther down the line can be put in.

I use 1/2-inch plastic pipe that is not rated safe for delivering drinking water and is therefore cheaper. It is fairly rigid plastic but can still be coiled up. The price for 100 feet varies considerably from store to store. Light-weight plastic garden hose can also be used; it compares favorably in price to the

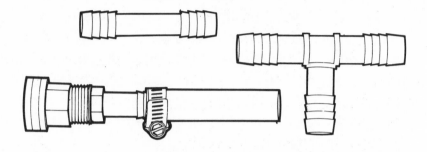

Fig. 4.1. Components of a drip irrigation system.
(Illustration by Susan Hunt.)

plastic pipe, and it comes complete with fittings at both ends.

Most likely, you'll hook up your system to a garden hose as I do. In hardware terminology, the end of the garden hose is a male connector. Your drip system needs to have a pivoting female connector with a rubber washer to provide a seal. I get the kind that is used to fix garden hoses; you push it into the pipe and secure it with a hose clamp. That's as complicated as it gets. To splice lengths of hose together, a straight piece of plastic fits tightly inside the plastic pipe and is secured with hose clamps on the two sections you are joining. If you decide to make your system more complicated, plastic connectors come in other shapes to form T's as shown in Figure 4.1. Push-on plastic caps with clamps keep the water from running merrily out the end of the pipe. There is so little pressure on the end of the system that I often just bend the pipe sharply and put on a hose clamp to keep it kinked. Baling wire also works in a pinch.

Laying Out the Drip System: I lay out the pipe next to the trees before I get too far along in putting things together. Since the plastic pipe shrinks and expands with temperature change, it is wise to allow extra footage, weaving it around the trees as in Figure 4.2 instead of stretching it out taut from end to end. That way the water-emitting hole will be approximately where it should be. As long as the emitter is within 12 inches of the plant, the water will get to the roots.

Commercial systems use emitters that deliver a certain amount of water at each point. This way the trees at the end of the line get the same amount of water as those near the source, which is difficult to accomplish in a large system. My systems are relatively short, so I don't worry about this and do not use emitters, although some trees may get a little extra water.

I make tiny holes in the plastic pipe with a boring tool. A tool that drills is better than one that pokes into the plastic because water pressure tends to close poked holes. Most of the holes are about 1/16 inch diameter so that the water squirts rather than drips. Since water pressure is greatest nearer the water source, I make the holes smaller there and enlarge them toward the end of the line. Pressure is also less on the uphill side if there is a change of elevation in the system; therefore, I sometimes put two holes by trees growing on the uphill end to even out the amount each tree receives.

I make the holes on the bottom of the plastic pipe so that it drains; eliminating the need to worry about water freezing and splitting the pipe over winter. I can leave the drip system in place year round. The pipe is often buried beneath the mulch; taking it up every fall would be a hassle.

The mulch protects the plastic from the ultraviolet rays of the sun and will extend its life considerably. The pipe is supposed to last five to seven years, but the mulch cover should keep it in good condition even longer. I can move the drip system to another location once the first set of trees is well established.

Drip Watering Rate: Leaving the system on for about three hours in our sandy loam soil makes a 12-inch circle of moisture around the tree. Experiment with your own system to see how long to water depending on water pressure and the size of the holes in your pipes. Place a gallon can under a drip hole to determine how long to leave your system running; this will eliminate guesswork.

Drip-System Maintenance: Every spring I flush the system by taking the end caps off and allowing the water to shoot straight through, flushing out the accumulated debris from the year before and unplugging the holes. A filter would minimize this accumulation. The use of emitters makes filters mandatory. The larger holes aren't quite so touchy, so I don't bother with filters. From time to time, I check to see if each tree is getting watered and simply poke a wire into the hole a few times to unclog any that aren't working. The system I've described is unsophisticated, but it works well. Perhaps its primitiveness is the best thing about it. It's cheap, easily fixed, reliable, and has no moving parts.

Drip-System Options: Emitters allow for a longer run of pipe and more watering points because you control exactly how much water is delivered at each point. I get around this by

Fig.4.2. Drip-system hose woven around trees.

making shorter runs and varying the sizes of the holes. This results in more water being applied to fewer trees at a time. Instead of watering the entire shelterbelt at once, you could water the pine row, for example, and then connect the hose to the drip line on the cedar row. The water source could come to the middle of the rows and your drip system could split to water half of a row at one time. When I was experimenting with drip systems, I watered the pine row and then moved the entire drip line to the cedar row. The trees need to be the same distance apart in the row in order for this to work, but it saves the expense of a duplicate line. It's a lot of hassle to do this though, and the drip line must be laid on top of any mulch in order to move the line. The water is not applied where it would do the most good, and the drip line is exposed to sunlight.

Using Drip-System Irrigation on Individually Grown Trees: Drip systems aren't limited to cultivated shelterbelts. I have trees tucked into unused corners all around our ranch buildings. Drip pipes are covered with the mulch so that the water never gets a chance to evaporate in a hot wind. I can hook a system up to the hydrant when I do chores and turn it off a few hours later. The job has taken me all of one minute, and the trees have been well watered. Actually, I seldom have to water because of the efficient way the water is applied and conserved.

When using a drip system in odd corners, remember that the plastic pipe doesn't stand up to being run over by vehicles and mowers. To avoid this, I sometimes bury the pipe beneath the sod between trees, leaving the emitter hole above ground to avoid clogging.

Drip-System Advantages: Drip-watered, well-mulched trees are carefree and not dependent on the tree grower having sufficient time to devote to their care. I have a row of mulched, drip-watered silver buffaloberries growing along the north side of our garden as a snow trap. Planted in a drought year, every single one grew and put out considerable growth. The best part was that I didn't need to do any more than hook up the hose now and then. The more trees I plant, the more I like setups like that. I plan to leave the drip system on the silver buffaloberries only a few years and then move it somewhere else. They should not need extra water longer than that because they are planted in a dead furrow that catches runoff from the corrals.

You can get quite sophisticated with drip irrigation. You can have a professional design your system, particularly if you plan to water an entire shelterbelt. Drip irrigation can run between one- and one-and-a-half dollars per tree for a shelterbelt system complete with debris-removing filters, water-pressure regulators, and water emitters.

Commercial Products

Anti-Transpirants

One of the best ways to conserve water in growing evergreens is a commercial anti-dessicant that reduces moisture loss through transpiration by coating the foliage. It comes in concentrated form and you mix it yourself to spray onto the tree foliage. It doesn't take the place of adequate water, but it helps reduce the stresses of wind and drought and is particularly helpful after transplanting. I wouldn't plant evergreens without using this type of product. Several brand names are available, although the nursery I use had to order it the first time I asked for it.

Cross-Linked Polyacrylamides

A commercial product that extends the time between waterings is cross-linked polyacrylamide, a water-absorbing polymer which can absorb up to 400 times its weight in deionized water. Absorption in actual use will depend on the salt content of the soil, but it definitely absorbs enough water to provide a reservoir of water for plants' use during times of drought. The polymer continues to absorb and release water in the soil for at least seven years, plenty of time for a tree to become established.

The polymer comes as a dry crystal. When added to water, it rehydrates and expands considerably in size to the consistency of chopped jello. The crystals can be placed in the planting hole dry or already hydrated. If they are used dry, an especially generous watering is needed in order to sufficiently hydrate the crystals to create a reservoir effect.

One advantage is that the expanding crystals enhance soil-to-root contact for the newly planted tree. However, I prefer to soak the crystals in water for 40 minutes before placing them in the planting hole because then I know that the tree has a reserve of moisture. Hydrating the polymer first is like putting a reserve of water beneath the roots for the seedlings to draw on as needed.

How much water is stored for the tree depends on how many polymer crystals are used. How many crystals to use depends on your goal in using it. If you intend only to enhance the survival rate of the tree, use just a few ounces of the dry material. If you want to accelerate first year growth and provide greater water storage for the plant, use four to eight ounces of dry polymer. This amount of polymer can eliminate the need for irrigation because the material absorbs moisture that would ordinarily gravitate below the reach of the plant's roots. Combining the polymer with use of a water catchment saucer or soil dam ensures that the crystals are rehydrated even with light rains. Greater amounts of polymer can be used if you want to store large amounts of water for a tree. As much as 25 to 250 gallons of water can be held in storage beneath a tree by increasing the amount of polymer.

Cost of cross-linked polyacrylamide is a small factor to consider when balanced against all of the benefits derived from its use. Water is conserved, irrigation costs are diminished, tree replacement costs are lower due to increased seedling survival, and growth is accelerated.

Establishing trees on sandy soil requires frequent irrigation because the water runs right past the roots into the subsoil. I had poor success getting seedlings established in sandy soil because the site was far from our ranch headquarters, making watering difficult. However, when I used pre-hydrated polymer crystals in the planting holes, survival and growth was doubled compared to trees planted without polymer. When I combined the use of the anti-transpirant spray, cross-linked polyacrylamide, and commercial, plastic tree shelters, an even greater survival and growth occurred in that difficult situation.

Plastic Tree Shelters

The tree shelters I use are wonderful inventions made from a double layer of UV-resistant, corrugated plastic formed into a circle. They come in diameters ranging from 3-1/4 to 4-1/2 inches so that four can be nested in shipment. Lengths vary from 2 to 6 feet to accommodate different tree heights. They are designed to last at least five to seven years and then degrade.

The tree shelter is placed over the newly planted seedling and pushed into the soil to a depth of one inch. The shelter is anchored with a strap attached to a stake driven into the ground. Because they completely enclose the young tree, the shelters create a "greenhouse effect" which serves to dramatically increase growth and increase survival rates. The tree draws moisture from the soil transpiring it into the air inside the shelter. The moisture condenses on the walls of the shelter, runs back down to the soil, and is available again for use by the tree. The tree waters itself. By protecting the tree inside from drying winds, the shelters provide even more benefit.

In addition to accelerating tree growth, shelters also provide protection from bark-nibbling rodents and grazing by livestock. They don't completely eliminate the need for fencing, however. Herbicide application is made easier with use of shelters because the herbicide can't penetrate the plastic wall.

Summary

Use of the methods discussed in this chapter will increase survival of seedlings. I advocate applying extra water only in the first few years of a tree's life. After that it should be able to seek and find its own water, especially if water-gathering and conservation techniques are used. The tree species makes a big difference in the ability of the tree to thrive without further irrigation. Selection of species that can withstand periods of little water is as critical as applying water when needed.

CHAPTER FIVE

Tough Species

Wanted: Industrial-strength trees. Must be able to survive inhospitable conditions: temperatures as low as -30° F and as high as 110° F, with breakneck changes between the two extremes; excruciating drought; wretched winds; faint humidity; and skimpy, rock-infested, and often briny soil. No wimps need apply.

Don't expect a flood of applicants. Where climate is warm, wet, and easy, just about any tree can fill the position; but where it is harsh, only the toughest survive. This doesn't leave a long list of trees to choose from. I grow 15 species on our ranch, which is a meager number compared to those that grow in milder areas. Maple, birch, hickory, beech, walnut, willow, linden, black locust, Canadian hemlock, and aspen are trees I admire in a glossy book. They are not ones that will survive without pampering on my dryland.

The plains offer so much in return that I don't begrudge this lack of cooperation. I'm happy with the 15 trees that do grow, and I am grateful for their tenacity, adaptability, and persistence. They don't shrivel at the first sign of drought; instead, they hunker down and survive. The sheer force of will and character of a cedar tree that has survived since homestead days is awesome; adversity shaped its branches but didn't win. That is the kind of tree I want to plant.

I've wasted a lot of time planting trees that didn't stand a chance of growing. I relied too heavily on the plant hardiness zone map often seen in catalogs and books, believing that if a particular tree was hardy to my zone it would indeed grow here. South Dakota is in zone four, but so is Minnesota, land of 10,000 lakes and a lot more rain. Many environmental factors can determine the favorability of a particular site. Moderate temperature, wind protection, good air, high humidity, good moisture conditions, adequate soil drainage, deep, fertile, correct soil conditions, and dependable snow cover for mulch can make a spot less harsh. Temperature is the only consideration on the plant hardiness zone map for determining a tree's hardiness. The rough conditions on my plains fall short of ideal in most of the other factors that make a site favorable; therefore, the zone map and nursery descriptions are misleading. They don't evaluate other factors important to trees' survival here.

Determining What Trees Will Survive

If catalogs and maps don't give recommendations based on the unique and critical climactic factors of the plains, how are you going to figure out what to plant?

Tough Species

Successful old trees in locations similar to yours are a good indicator of the kind of tree to plant. If you see no maples in the neighborhood, consider it a bad omen for growing maples. The trees that survive in neglected old shelterbelts or farmsteads are an excellent choice because you know they are tough. In studying neighborhood trees, be alert for special conditions that enabled the tree to survive. If you can't duplicate those conditions, weigh the choice carefully. For instance, an unusually high water table in a draw or spring-fed hillside can support vigorous tree growth that is not possible on more typical upland prairie.

My aim in tree planting is not to see if I can grow an exotic type not recommended for my area. By creating an artificially favorable microclimate, I might be able to grow more delicate trees, but I don't want to do that. Every successful entity on this prairie is tenacious; toughness and the ability to endure are essential in order to survive in this harsh environment. To plant trees that are mere pansies in a place like this is absolute foolishness. The sissies take more resources to grow and are more apt to squander all that effort by failing anyway. Choose the toughest trees you can find, and they will reward both you and future generations.

I don't always follow the principle outlined above. I have pet trees in addition to the 15 tough ones: 19 lovely Black Hills spruce. Nature grows spruce trees on cool north-facing slopes within sound of a picturesque mountain stream; their shallow sissy roots need water right at their toes all the time. You'll not find a spruce tree on a dry hill, except at my house, or those of other admirers of spruce trees who are willing to coddle, pamper, and protect.

Growing Trees on the Great Plains

My spruce trees grow in a double row north of our house where they protect us from wind and make heating easier in winter. Pine trees would serve the purpose as well, but spruce have majesty and grace that are hard to resist. A thick pine-needle mulch blankets the soil, concealing a 1/2-inch plastic pipe that is part of the drip irrigation system that helps keep them alive on my hillside. Such extravagance can be afforded in a small area because it is within easy reach of a garden hose. If I were to neglect their care during dry years, they would soon suffer. Understand that I limit my pet trees to the yard where I can take care of them.

I hesitate to list the trees that do well for me in this particular corner of the plains. Other types may be more suited for you in your corner. Different trees and shrubs are recommended for other parts of the plains that I have no experience growing. I won't write about them. The 15 tough trees that I grow are adapted over a wide area of the dry part of the Great Plains and are certainly worth your consideration.

Use common sense in determining which trees match your conditions, however. Perhaps you live in a slightly wetter area than I do and can grow more moisture-loving trees. It's impossible to say that a certain tree requires a certain minimum amount of moisture per year because it would fail to take into account all of the other factors that determine survivability. While it's good to plant stalwart types of trees and shrubs, it's also worthwhile to try some of the types that you're not sure of. Try them on a small scale; if they prove successful, plant more.

Portfolio
of my
Fifteen
Favorite Trees

Tree illustrations
for portfolio by Susan Hunt.

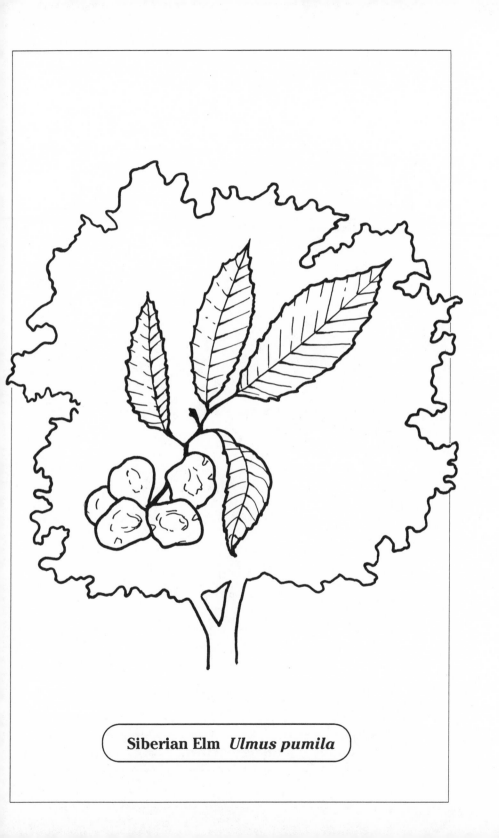

Siberian Elm *Ulmus pumila*

Common Hackberry *Celtis occidentalis*

Honeylocust *Gleditsia triacanthos*

Green Ash *Fraxinus pennsylvanica*

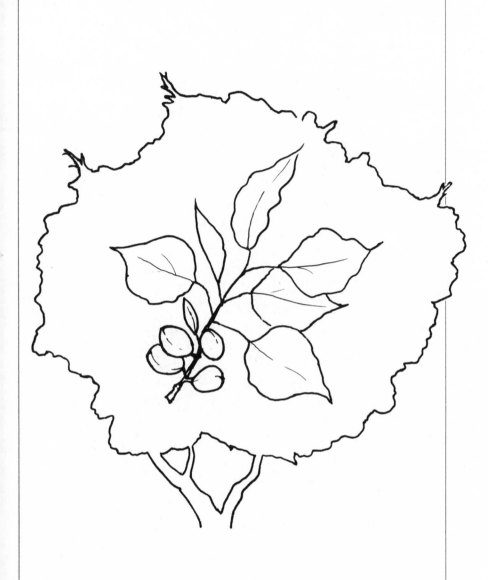

Manchurian Apricot *Prunus armeniaca,*
var. *mandshurica*

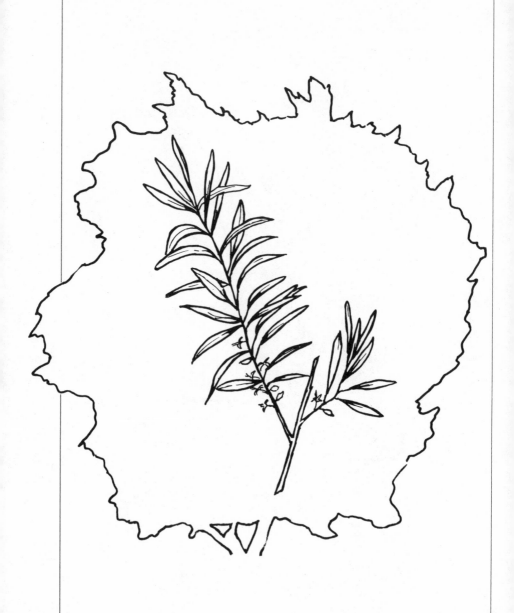

Russian Olive *Elaeagnus angustifolia*

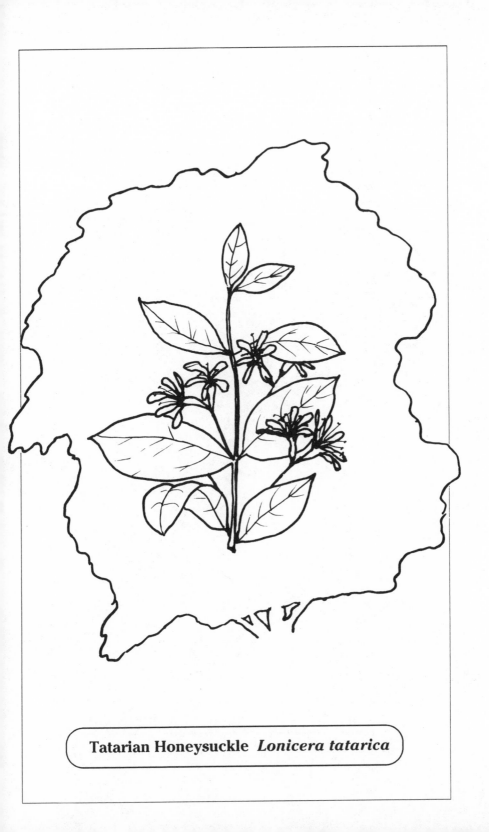

Tatarian Honeysuckle *Lonicera tatarica*

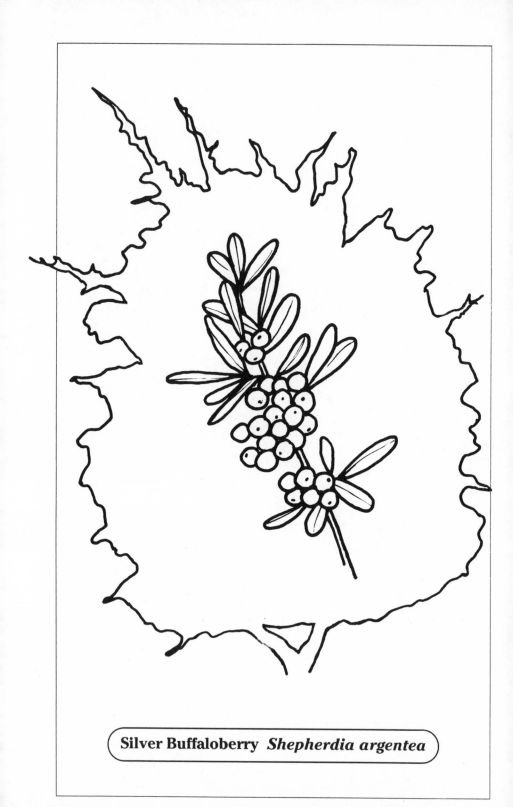

Silver Buffaloberry *Shepherdia argentea*

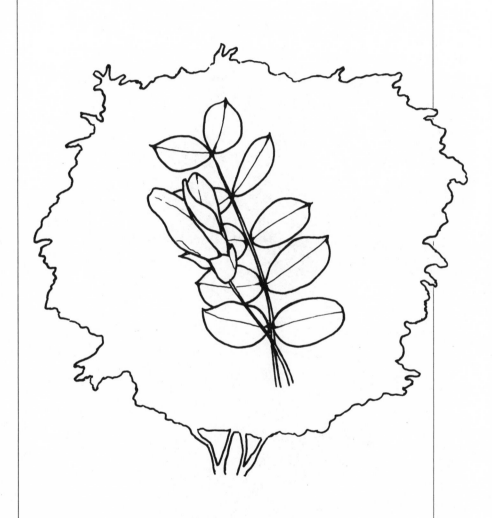

Siberian Peashrub *Caragana arborescens*

Common Lilac *Syringa vulgaris*

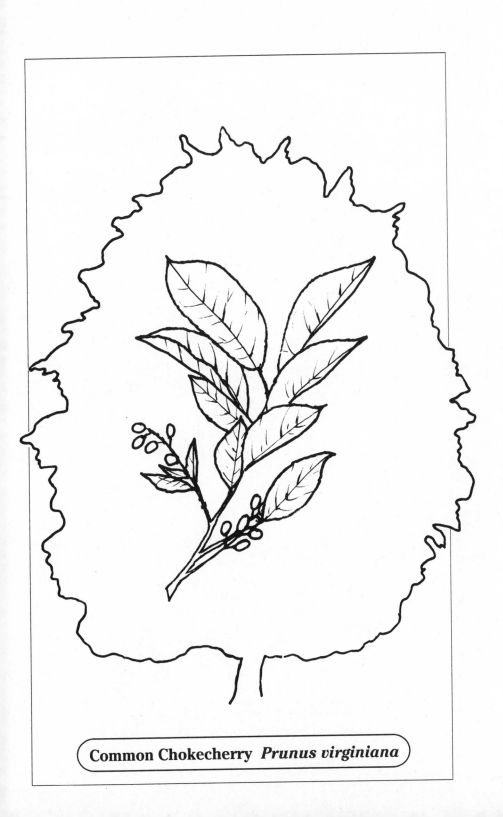

Common Chokecherry *Prunus virginiana*

American Plum *Prunus americana*

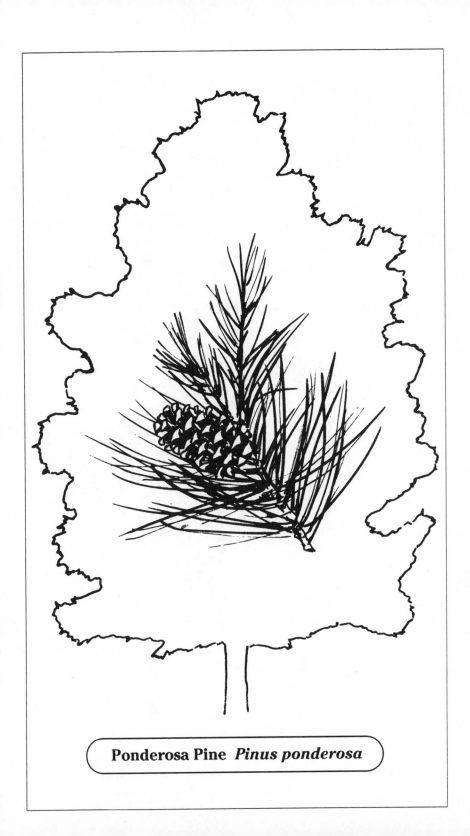

Ponderosa Pine *Pinus ponderosa*

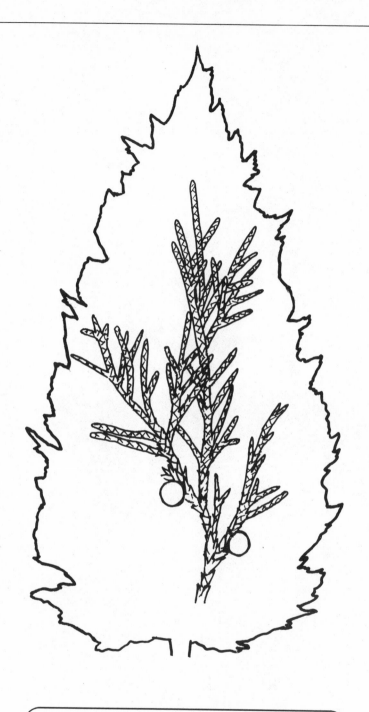

Eastern Red Cedar *Juniperus virginiana*

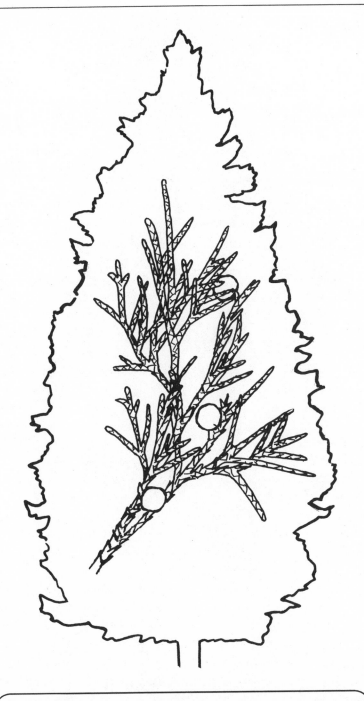

Rocky Mountain Juniper *Juniperus scopulorum*

My Fifteen Favorite Trees

Tall Deciduous

Siberian Elm *Ulmus pumila*: People who can grow maples and willows consider Siberian elm a weed tree; those of us who have a hard time growing anything at all call it a reliable old standby. It transplants easily, quickly grows to usable size, and is as tough as they come. The Siberian elm is not fussy about soil or alkali conditions, so it adapts over a wide range. Siberian elm is a good tree for dry locations because it can survive on an annual rainfall as low as 10 inches and is extremely cold hardy. However, its habit of blooming and budding early in spring make it susceptible to late winter cold snaps. The trees suffer die-back, but they put out new growth nonetheless.

Siberian elm grows quickly. It is often used in windbreaks to provide protection for slower-growing species that are becoming established. Depending on the location and growing conditions, it will be 25 to 35 feet tall and 20 feet wide in 20 years. It has a life span of 30 to 40 years, relatively short compared to some other species. Crowding further reduces its life span. Siberian elm is frequently planted as a temporary tree, so this feature can be used to advantage. If planted with pines, for instance, the elms are declining about the time that the pines are reaching their prime.

One distinct disadvantage, roots of Siberian elm are so shallow and wide-spreading that they compete with crops or other nearby trees. On the other hand, I have noticed that the weed creeping jenny does not flourish beneath Siberian elm. I can't explain why, but I am delighted. This effect seems to extend in a circle under the entire canopy.

This tree is resistant to Dutch elm disease but is affected by canker problems and elm leaf beetles that feed heavily on the leaves. The larval stage of this beetle does most of the actual leaf damage; adult beetles overwinter in cozy places beneath the bark of firewood or in attics. The insects skeletonize the elm leaves. Although the trees don't seem to be severely harmed by them, the infestation, coupled with additional stress such as drought, has the potential to kill the tree. A biological control is available.

If you intend to use chemicals to control weeds or plan to grow elms near a field in which herbicides are used, you should know that elm is extremely sensitive to 2,4-D.

Although a Siberian elm's tenacity is admirable, its twigs and branches are brittle and tend to shed after every storm. This isn't a problem in the back forty, but you will have a steady job picking up twigs beneath an elm in your yard. The seeds are another drawback. Some years create conditions perfect for seed production, and bushels of them flutter down to form drifts on the sidewalk. Elm seedlings can be the worst weed in the garden, although they seldom take root in undisturbed soil.

Despite the Siberian elm's lack of ornamental value, it is a much-planted species for the simple reason that it grows despite adverse conditions and with little care. In South Dakota, 50 percent of city and small town trees are Siberian elm. It occupies many shelterbelt rows in rural areas as well. In the early years of tree plantings on our ranch, half of the trees we planted were elm because we wanted quick-growers that would provide shelter immediately. In later years we tried to diversify our plantings with a variety of longer-lived trees to avoid problems in case disease or insects should wipe out the elms. We credit the wind protection provided by the elms for making subsequent plantings easier to establish.

Common Hackberry *Celtis occidentalis*: The hackberry offers everything I want in a tree: long-lived, strong-limbed, drought-resistant, deep-rooted, and easily adapted to a wide range of soils. And its berries feed the birds.

I've read that seed source is especially important to the hardiness of hackberry and that young trees are subject to winter injury. I've never had any trouble with mine. I've also read that they are slow-growing on dry sites. Mine have put out 18 inches of growth in many dry years. Apparently those deep roots found some moisture I didn't know about.

Hackberries grow in the tall rows of my shelterbelts where they provide good protection for long distances downwind and can tolerate shading from trees nearby. I've also planted them in the houseyard because they are an attractive tree, and their 30- to 40-foot height and crown width make a lot of shade. The hackberry doesn't shed twigs, and its strong limbs won't crash into the house during a wind storm. I've never had any problems with hackberry, but they are subject to witches broom, which is a branch deformation, and nipple gall, which grows on foliage.

Honeylocust *Gleditsia triacanthos:* Honeylocust is a nitrogen factory; its classification as a legume means that it extracts this valuable element from the air and adds it to the soil. There is such a thing as "a free lunch" after all.

If you hate to rake leaves, honeylocust is the tree for

your yard. Its leaves are so tiny that they disappear with the wind before they hit the ground. They do not cast a dense shade with those little leaves either. A honeylocust tree doesn't seem to have enough branches; it wastes no energy growing a lot of twigs to fill in the spaces of its canopy, so consequently a honeylocust tree in winter isn't a great snow-stopper. It does contribute some upper level density to a shelterbelt and makes an excellent field windbreak.

With their delicate, lacy foliage honeylocusts seem almost out of place in this harsh country, but that ferny look hides a tree full of mean thorns. The thorns don't bother me, because I don't climb trees or build tree houses anymore. If I did, I'd plant a thornless selection. These have the disadvantage of being less hardy and more susceptible to disease, however. I say plant the toughest kind of honeylocust and climb only hackberry trees.

A honeylocust tree enjoys a moderately long life, growing from 30 to 50 feet tall and equally wide. It will tolerate annual precipitation of only 12 inches, grows on alkali soil fairly well, but may have problems with canker in stressful situations. My honeylocusts have grown beautifully in one of our shelterbelts for 15 years, but they have had only drought to contend with. No doubt drought combined with alkali soils would be more stressful.

Green Ash *Fraxinus pennsylvanica:* Green ash used to be one of my favorite large trees; but since many of mine are now dying from borer attacks, I've moved it to the bottom of my list. The particular borer that enjoys green ash trees drills holes into the trunks of drought-stressed trees and larval feeding eventually kills them. However, many suckers from the root make a green ash "bush." Since most of my trees are drought-stressed at one time or another, borers are hard to avoid. The trees seem to be able to survive on dry soils quite well; but if the borer is going to kill them anyway, this drought resistance is not very valuable. No doubt there are numerous methods to kill the insects, but I think it is wiser to plant trees that have no major insect problems, especially when planting large quantities or in situations where you can't pamper them.

For this reason, I plant green ash only in my most favorable locations: where they get runoff from a road, where the gutter delivers extra water, or in a low spot that collects water from a large area. Green ash can survive in standing water for 50 days, significant information if you were considering planting one at the edge of a dam where water may stand during the wet part of the year.

In dry country, green ash reach a mature height of 30 to 40 feet, with a 25-foot canopy spread. They transplant well. Although they grow slowly in their early years, they put out more rapid growth as they get older. Green ash is considered a long-lived tree—if they survive the borers. 'Marshall's Seedless' is a male cultivar that has fewer insect problems but may not be available in the quantities or sizes you'd want for shelterbelts.

The deep root system of green ash make it valuable as a tree for crop protection because it doesn't compete with the crop for moisture as much as shallow-rooted trees do.

Medium-Sized Deciduous

Manchurian Apricot *Prunus armeniaca*, var. *mandshurica*: Manchurian apricot is one of the few kinds of trees that survived in my father's shelterbelt after cultivation was abandoned. The trees grew to at least 15 feet tall and 15 feet wide in the 35 years that they lived; half that time they were not cultivated. A tough few still survive. The trees produced fruit only once in their early years because they bloomed so early in the spring that their blossoms froze.

This is a tree that I plant just because it looks so good. I enjoy the bonsai-like form of its spreading branches and crooked trunks. We have planted seven Manchurian apricot trees along our driveway; they are widely spaced so that the beauty of each tree can be appreciated.

Russian Olive *Elaeagnus angustifolia:* Some of my favorite comedy happens right outside my living room window when the sharp-tailed grouse are having lunch in the Russian olive trees in the shelterbelt across the road. The olive berries hang all along the branches right up to the tips, so the grouse sits on the branch and yanks berries off as he scoots up the branch. The comedy begins when the branch is no longer able to support the weight of the grouse as he sidles toward the tip and falls off. He is still hungry, so he flies back up to the same branch tip, which has not gotten any stronger in the 30 seconds since he's been there last. Amid much wing flapping and clucking, he finally finds a branch that can just barely hold his weight and resumes lunch. Multiply this performance by four grouse in the same tree and you have a show worth buying tickets for.

We planted our first Russian olives because we wanted a dense tree to stop the snow and wind for our cattle and around our buildings. The ones we plant now are for the sharp-tailed grouse and birds. The original purpose still is fulfilled; their dense canopy provides protection for cattle and buildings at the same time that it shelters and feeds wildlife.

The silver-green foliage of Russian olive is pleasant to look at and the little blossoms have a pungent but pleasing smell that I look forward to every spring. Nice as this tree is to see and smell, I admire it most because it is such a savvy, surviving kind of plant complete with thorns. Most other tree species produce a single trunk and let weeds crowd right up to the bark, but Russian olive spreads its canopy inches off the ground and chases the weeds farther away with each year's growth. This is the ultimate in weed control: let the tree do it. They provide their own weed suppression very quickly and their growth rate is extraordinary with good care.

Russian olive fits into many tree-growing situations. As a shelterbelt tree it is first rate. It grows to a height of 20 to 25 feet and a width of 15 to 20 feet, with good snow-stopping capacity. Since it grows so rapidly, it provides wind-slowing action at a very young age when other trees are still getting established. It is not, however, extremely long-lived. As the tree ages, the lower crown tends to become open, especially if it has been crowded and shaded by taller trees. Most of our Russian olives are in our shelterbelt rows, but we also have some planted in clusters in the corners of the shelterbelts where they provide still more grouse food and protection.

Like any tree, Russian olive has good points and bad. It adapts to alkaline soil and a wide range of moisture conditions, including drought. However it is susceptible to disease problems that weaken the tree. The low-growing canopy takes a beating from cultivation equipment; this stress encourages diseases to invade. The wood is weak, and some diseases—notably canker—weaken the tree even further, making it even more subject to "disk disease," or cultivation damage.

I have some trouble with the ends of the branches dying back in winter. It doesn't seem to matter if the year has been wet or dry. The tree recovers well the next summer, however. During the mid-1940s a Russian olive dieback disease was quite common, and it is still present in some dryland plantings. Apparently this is what affects my trees. But I've never lost one on account of this disease, and I still continue to plant Russian olive because I need the laughs they and the grouse provide.

Low-Growing Deciduous
Tatarian Honeysuckle *Lonicera tatarica:* Honeysuckle is the bush with beautiful red, but extra-strength sour berries. As children we loved to fool our friends with them. We'd marvel at how delicious they were until our victim tasted one. Then we'd collapse in fits of laughter at the puckered face. Birds must have an altered sense of taste because they seem to love honeysuckle berries in summer and the fall, as long as the berries hang on the bushes.

We have a partial row of honeysuckle in one shelterbelt that has grown into a dense wall in spite of some very dry years. They give excellent ground-level protection, grow rapidly, and are easy to establish even in alkaline soils. Eventually, they should reach a height and width of 10 feet.

The Russian aphid is becoming a more widespread pest of this bush every year. The insect sucks the plant's juices from the underside of the leaves, making the leaves crinkle and curl as if in agony. The affected leaves are mostly at the branch tips; and they remain on the bush all winter, so you need only look for clusters of dead leaves to detect the aphid's handiwork after the rest of the leaves have fallen. Cutting and burning these dead leaves will help to control the insect. In Minnesota and Wisconsin the aphid eventually kills the bush after two to three years of infestation. Mine have had aphids for several years and continue to grow well. Insecticides are available to kill the aphid, but it's wiser to do nothing if your bushes aren't suffering from the attack and give nature some time to work out the problem herself. Sometimes a pest builds up until a predator population catches up and gets things under control. Check out the honeysuckle in your area; if they are free of aphids, or surviving well in spite of them, it would be safe to include this valuable shrub in your plantings. If they are being killed by the insects it would be better to avoid honeysuckle altogether, or to plant the aphid-resistant variety known as *Lonicera maackii*.

Silver Buffaloberry *Shepherdia argentea:* Buffaloberry grows wild on our prairie, so we know it's tough enough to survive in our domestic plantings. I believe it is one of the most drought-tolerant and cold-hardy plants available. It doesn't seem to be fussy about soil, even tolerating alkaline conditions. It chooses rough, rocky places to grow wild, so it's no wonder that it's done well wherever I've planted it. Buffaloberry has the ability to take nitrogen from the air to use in photosynthesis, enabling it to not only survive in poor soil but to actually improve it.

Buffaloberry doesn't get as tall as Russian olive, but its

silver-gray leaves and small inconspicuous flowers are very similar to it. Actually I prefer this shrub to Russian olive because it is even denser and has no dieback problems. Buffaloberry only grows to 10 feet tall and 7 feet wide, but that amounts to 490 cubic feet of excellent bush.

Apparently tough trees and shrubs gain some feeling of strength by growing thorns; most have them, including buffaloberry. On the buffaloberry they protect the delicious orange-red berries that make wonderful, but hard-earned, jam. This shrub does not bear fruit every year, probably because it blooms so early that the flowers freeze in early spring cold snaps.

Siberian Peashrub *Caragana arborescens:* The only negative thing I can say about Siberian peashrub is that I didn't plant more of them years ago. They make quick growth on very little precipitation, do well in alkaline soil, and are easy to transplant and establish. Siberian peashrub reach their full size of 8 feet tall and 8 feet wide in as little as 10 years. They are excellent in the shrub row of a shelterbelt because they trap snow at a young age. Their medium-dense crown is vase shaped, with most of the foliage in the upper half of the shrub. They can be pruned to the ground after the first year of growth to promote more branching and lower density.

Siberian peashrub is one of the most widely planted shrubs because of its ability to adapt to a variety of growing situations. Siberian peashrub is not a shrub that you will need to coddle, spray, or pamper in order for it to grow; it is resistant to diseases. As a member of the legume family, it is not dependent on fertile soil to grow well. Aphids and grasshoppers enjoy a meal of Siberian peashrub sap and foliage, but the shrub never seems to notice the damage and just keeps on growing.

Common Lilac *Syringa vulgaris:* The smell of lilac blossoms in spring feeds the soul; that's reason enough to plant them. Aside from their beauty, they are a long-lived and dependable shrub that is a good addition to shelterbelt or houseyard. Their density at ground level provides good snow-trapping action. Even though they don't produce any food for wildlife, the protection from wind that they provide is equally valuable. Their mature height will vary from 6 to 15 feet, depending on moisture conditions. Their width continues to increase as the suckers grow from the base, eventually expanding to 6 to 8 feet across. The suckers can be separated from the parent plant and transplanted to another location with good success, especially if done before the buds break in spring. Lilacs are slow growers but have excellent drought tolerance. Lilac borers can be a problem, but the shrub has virtually no diseases. Don't plan to use herbicides around lilacs because they are very sensitive to chemicals.

Common Chokecherry *Prunus virginiana:* You'll soon have your larder full of jelly, fruit leather, and wine if you plant chokecherry bushes in any quantity at all. When you run out of ways to use them, the birds will be enthusiastic harvesters of the glossy black berries. Be sure to wait until the berries reach this dark color, otherwise you will understand how they got their name; they are tolerably sweet only when they are ripe.

Chokecherry blossoms have such a delicately sweet fragrance that we find it hard to resist gathering a bouquet for the house. Both chokecherries and wild plums bloom early in the spring at a time when flowers are a rare treat. As beekeepers, we are always aware of when these two bloom because they are excellent nectar yielders for both domestic and wild bees.

Chokecherry's habit of suckering by underground runners fills in areas between the original plants and creates a solid hedge in a few years. If suckers pop up between the rows or in a neighboring row, you can either leave them to add density or transplant them to a bare spot. They will grow to 10 feet tall and nearly as wide on very little moisture. The fact that they are so dense allows them to get by on less actual rainfall because they can trap enough snow to add several inches to their moisture stores.

Chokecherry is susceptible to fire blight, a bacterial disease that makes the ends of shoots look as if they've been scorched by fire. I've never had any trouble with this, but you should watch for it. It can be very troublesome because it is spread by wind and pollinating insects.

I have problems with webworms. They make huge webs in both chokecherry and plum bushes and then eat all the foliage within the web. They can denude an entire branch by the time I notice their web woven among the leaves and branches. I cut the branch and web out, haul it home in a bucket and burn it in the wood stove. I'm not sure this does any good because I have to do it every year, but it makes me feel like I'm keeping the worms under control.

American Plum *Prunus americana:* American or wild plum is a native tree east of the Rockies. It is very similar to chokecherry in growth habit and size. Sucker growth from the shallow roots provide quick wind protection and snow trapping. It also has problems with fire blight and webworms.

Wild plum is a good bush to plant in a shelterbelt or as a separate thicket. It not only provides food and cover for wildlife but for your household as well. The fruit can be quite sweet or unbelievably sour, both on the same bush. I love to walk through the shelterbelts and reap a pocketful of sweet wild plums to munch on for the rest of my tour.

Tall Evergreen

Ponderosa Pine *Pinus ponderosa:* I plant ponderosa pine because this species is a native here; the Black Hills are covered with millions of excellent specimens. About 35 species of pine are native to North America, with only 13 of those species native to the east and south. The remaining ones are found in the west. Ponderosa grows naturally in such wide-ranging places as South Dakota, Oregon, Colorado, northern Arizona, and New Mexico, from elevations of 2,000 to 9,000 feet. Your state's tree nursery will offer the type of pine adapted to your area.

When you plant and grow a pine tree, you can be reasonably sure that it will be there for a good long time. A pine on my parents' land was cut at the wonderful age of 288 years by actual count of the rings. It first shouldered its way up through the pine duff beneath its mother tree in 1680, about the same time the 13 colonies were being established 2,000 miles away. Life was not all easy for the tree; its rings show drought years and wetter ones. Scars in the rings tell of a fire, probably caused by lightning, at the time Lewis and Clark explored this territory. At that time it was no sapling but a 192-year-old giant. About the time that the Civil War was scorching the South another fire badly damaged one side of the tree and left a charred gap. The whistle of the first train that went through this part of Dakota Territory in 1886 reverberated through its trunk; the sounds of cars and trucks on the highway or the first airplane overhead must have been a strange vibration after centuries of only wind in its branches.

The long life of a ponderosa pine makes it ideal for shelterbelt planting because it will reach mature size about the time the shorter-lived trees are dwindling. Evergreens in general grow more slowly than broadleaf trees in their first 10 years; after that the growth rates are nearly the same. Combining pine with a more quickly growing deciduous tree is a good idea because you get the windbreak you want sooner and keep it for a longer time. Pine will give good density only at middle and upper levels in a shelterbelt because they tend to loose their lower branches as shade from other trees increases. They need full sun to develop a dense crown, and the thick stands of a shelterbelt setting usually don't offer this. Thinning the trees before they begin to lose lower branches will help prevent the loss of lower limbs.

Ponderosa isn't terribly fussy about its soil, even tolerating some alkaline conditions. Drought obviously doesn't bother pine trees because they seem to do their best in their native habitat on a hot, south-facing slope. They are seldom found growing in the valleys. The key to their drought resistance is their long taproot; four-year-old trees may have taproots 4 to 5 feet long, although moderately deep, wide-spreading laterals develop as the trees get older.

Pines are subject to a wide variety of diseases and insects, but that doesn't mean that yours will have all of them. The only problem I've encountered with mine is pine tip moth, an insect that burrows into next year's bud and kills it. This has the same effect as pinching out the bud; the next spring the tree merely grows two or more new shoots where the bud was, making the tree bushier. There is a chemical that will control the insect, but it is not practical for use on a large number of trees. Planting one of the varieties resistant to pine tip moth would be a better alternative. If the pest doesn't severely damage the tree, I see no reason to worry about it.

Mountain pine beetles are a problem in the Black Hills, but my actively growing young trees should not be in danger of attack. Such trees have an abundance of sap with which to drown out any invading beetles, one more reason to keep my trees healthy and growing well.

I love the pine fragrance in the still evening air around our house. Pines are one of the most reliable trees we've planted. Their year-round density keeps them on the job both summer and winter, protecting livestock and giving homes to wildlife.

Medium-Growing Evergreen

Eastern Red Cedar *Juniperus virginiana:* I'm naturally suspicious of any tree with "eastern" in its name. It conjures up images of a tree that would faint if rain failed to fall every other day. Actually "cedar" is a misnomer anyway because this is actually a juniper, as its scientific name indicates.

Eastern red cedar is native to the eastern half of the United States, where it excels in moist, loamy soil. It has adapted to areas of lesser rainfall as well, getting along on as little as 10 to 20 inches of precipitation per year due to its deep taproot. Of course, the tree won't grow as tall on that amount of rainfall. It reaches only 10 feet tall and 9 feet wide in 20 years. Mature heights will vary with moisture conditions, but the ones I've seen around here are under 20 feet. Wildlife enjoys the berries of the Eastern red cedar, and drinkers of gin appreciate the flavor the berries lend to that beverage.

Rocky Mountain Juniper *Juniperus scopulorum:* Rocky Mountain juniper is a native of western South Dakota. I know it's likely to do as well in the future as it has for centuries. Juniper growing on the hot, dry slopes of the Badlands of South Dakota don't look coddled to me. They look like the kind of tree that I want to grow, tough and durable.

The 20-year height of Rocky Mountain juniper will be approximately 12 feet, with a 9-foot width. Ultimate height will be somewhat taller, with a width reaching 12 feet or more. They do well on as little as 8 inches of precipitation per year, making a slow to moderate rate of growth.

Eastern red cedar and Rocky Mountain juniper are often used interchangeably where a medium-growing evergreen is desired to break the wind and drop snow for livestock or wildlife protection. Both have an exceptionally dense growth habit.

Both red cedar and Rocky Mountain juniper are alternate hosts to cedar-apple rust, a fungal disease that requires the presence of both host species in order to complete its life cycle. If apple trees grow within a quarter mile of your cedars or junipers, you should be on the lookout for the fleshy orange galls that are the fruiting spores of cedar-apple rust. Treatment is possible, but it may be wiser to put distance between the two types of trees unless you plant 'Medora,' a variety of Rocky Mountain juniper resistant to cedar-apple rust.

The abundant berries of both species attract cedar waxwings in droves. They swoop in, gorge their crops, make fools of themselves in general, and leave as quickly as they come. It's always a treat when they grace our trees with their presence; they decorate them better than any Christmas tree has ever been trimmed. I've been able to photograph them up close because they are more intent on gleaning every last berry on the tree than worrying about a lady with a camera.

Red cedar and Rocky Mountain juniper both are long-lived trees; the maximum age for Eastern red cedar is 300 years. A harsh climate can take years off the life span, but both trees can still be classified as extremely durable. Many have survived from homestead days, long after the shanties that they protected have gone.

Rocky Mountain juniper is larger and more drought-tolerant than red cedar, although it grows more slowly. Bare-root juniper stock has a poorer survival rate, making red cedar easier to establish. This is an important point since bare root is the usual type of stock available. If you provide supplemental watering, shade, and protection from hot winds in the first years, your trees will be able to return that protection to you over their long life span.

Often the leaders of both types of trees break under snow pressure, although this is less common with Rocky Mountain juniper. Red cedar tends to keep its lower branches better, especially when grown in an open, uncrowded situation. This factor is particularly important when depending on a low-growing evergreen for density, such as when grown with pine that lose their lower branches.

Eastern red cedar is more tolerant of alkaline soil than Rocky Mountain juniper. The latter has fair tolerance to alkalinity as well as to high water levels that usually exist with hardpan. Both types adapt to a wide range of soil types. With good care both will succeed in a variety of situations. Either tree is a good choice.

Diversity in Tree Plantings

The greatest risk in investing, whether it be in stocks or trees, is to put all your assets in one basket. Diversity reduces the gamble that you will lose everything. Plant as many different species of trees as will grow in your area to reduce the likelihood of suddenly finding yourself without any trees. An example of this is the many shelterbelts in South Dakota consisting largely of Siberian elm, normally an extremely hardy and drought-resistant tree. Persistent drought in the 1980s weakened the trees, and elm leaf beetle infestations were severe. On top of these stresses, unseasonably warm winters followed by arctic cold fronts killed swelling buds and as much as 75 percent of the crowns of trees. Most survived, but they were in a severely weakened and unattractive state; had the drought continued, they might have died. More than one rancher with shelterbelts consisting solely of Siberian elm wished that they contained more of a variety of tree species.

While planting many different species in a shelterbelt

prevents total failure of the planting when one species dies out, that doesn't mean that every other tree must be a different variety. In fact, all the trees in a row should be the same species; if the whole species fails, it will be easier to replace one complete row than to fill in scattered trees. Using one species to a row makes for more uniform width to the tree rows and makes planning distance between rows easier. Each row should be of a different species, however, so that the shelterbelt will continue to provide protection even if one row is unsuccessful.

The exception to this one-species-to-a-row rule is a one-row shelterbelt. Here two species can be combined to make a better windbreak, but the two must be compatible in growth habit. Hackberry and Siberian peashrub are a good team because the tall hackberry provides upper-level density while the Siberian peashrub fills in at lower levels. On the other hand, a deciduous tree, such as Siberian elm, planted with an evergreen, such as pine, will result in the faster-growing elm crowding out the evergreen.

CHAPTER SIX

Stock Acquisition, Planting, and Renovation

Good tree plantings don't just happen, especially not here in a semiarid region. They take planning, preparation, appropriate care techniques, and a lot of work. They take the kind of dedication to their care that comes from the love of trees and an appreciation of the benefits they provide.

My neighbor has one of the neatest, cleanest shelterbelts I've ever seen. It is truly a masterpiece. It can be seen from the highway and I admire its five straight, weedless rows every time I pass by. In the first years of the planting, I'd often see my neighbor, water tank in the back of his pickup, giving his trees a drink. The amount of work that has gone into nurturing such a beautiful set of trees deserves a medal. My neighbor would probably agree. In fact, he's semi-jokingly said that if he'd known what a lot of work they'd be, he'd never have planted them. I have thought the same thing about my own trees at times.

My neighbor's shelterbelt is planted upwind of his driveway where it will stop the snow within its rows and keep his road clear. If I ask him this winter during a blizzard if he's glad he planted those trees, I think I know his answer. Then no amount of hoeing and watering will have been too much to pay for a clear driveway. He'll be out there weeding and cultivating next summer, too. As his trees mature they'll be even more of an asset. They'll attract song birds and wildlife, decrease his home heating costs, increase weight gains in his cattle, and add thousands of dollars to the value of his property. I wouldn't be surprised if his present shelterbelt is only his first.

I got hooked the same way. Our ranch's original seven trees and shrubs were totally inadequate, so we planted one shelterbelt after another until we ran out of room. My husband claims we'll have to buy more land if we plant any more trees. My hope is that you also will see the value of trees and decide to plant as many as you can care for.

The basic care outlined in the previous chapters will assure the best chance of survival possible for your trees. You're going to deposit moisture into your trees' "waterbank" through summerfallow, water-catchment systems, and water-absorbing polymer. By planting only drought-resistant species, you'll be making sure that your trees aren't "spendthrifts" and won't require huge "withdrawals" from that bank. Cultivation and mulch will ensure that your trees will be the only ones making withdrawals, not waterbank-robbing weeds, because when trees are overdrawn at the waterbank, they're soon "no-account" trees. Using these techniques will give your trees a good healthy balance and a solid foundation for long life.

This chapter will highlight several more factors that contribute to initial survival and longevity of a tree planting. In reality, they are no less essential than those previously mentioned. First I'll discuss the best ways to acquire planting stock and do the actual planting. No tree planting will last long if animals have access to the trees, so I'll explain ways to protect from animal damage. Renovation will be covered last, although this important aspect begins soon after initial planting.

Stock Acquisition

The National Arbor Day Foundation's book *Arbor Day*, states that over a tree's 50-year lifetime, it generates $31,250 worth of oxygen, provides $62,000 worth of air pollution control, recycles $37,500 worth of water, and controls $31,250 worth of soil erosion. When the benefits of a tree are measured in dollars, the price of the seedling becomes less of an issue. Spending a few cents more per tree to get good quality pays in the long run.

The real cost of a tree is the money it takes to get it to survive and grow. If you get cheap, poor-quality stock you will not save money when the tree fails to grow and must be replaced. You've lost money and, worse yet, tree-growing time. Real economy is buying the best tree for the money; false economy is buying a tree that costs the least.

The best advice I can give on finding a good source of planting stock is to ask successful tree growers in your local area where they get their seedlings. You will benefit by their experiences, both good and bad, and save yourself from having to repeat their mistakes.

Nearly every plains state has its own nursery that supplies seedlings directly to conservation districts for private citizens to use in conservation plantings. This is my first recommendation for seedlings. Call the local office of the Soil Conservation Service to get information on placing an order. The trees they offer are ones adapted for each area, an advantage that commercial nurseries do not offer. The only problem is that you may have to order a minimum number of trees that may be more than you need. Generally, these numbers are ideal for shelterbelt planting. If you need only a few, locate a neighbor who also needs a small number of trees. Orders must be placed the fall before planting to ensure availability, so plan ahead.

My second choice for acquiring planting stock is to use volunteer seedlings. One summer, Siberian peashrub seedlings covered the ground beneath our shelterbelt bushes like thick clover. I tranplanted clumps of tiny plants into large pots, thinned them to one per pot after they had recovered from the shock of transplanting, and put them where I could water them easily. The next year when I needed Siberian peashrubs, I had some ready to transplant to a new location. Wild plums, chokecherries, lilacs, and even honeylocusts send up suckers from the roots or crowns of the plants. These can be dug up and transplanted in early spring before the leaves emerge.

Transplanting native tree seedlings from a nearby area is an option. I have the best success with ponderosa pine when I transplant them from my parents' ranch a mile away. I select trees that are already growing in the open sunlight and whisk them home to their new growing site in less than an hour. A large root ball comes along, complete with soil. The accompanying soil can be important, especially to evergreens, because plants often have a symbiotic relationship with fungi in the soil which helps the plant grow better. The trees have the "home soil advantage" in getting established.

Know what you're digging. If the trees are broadleaf, they won't have the leaves by which to identify them in early spring before bud-break. Don't dig them after the leaves appear because the survival rate will be drastically reduced. You'll either need to mark them the summer before or become an expert at identifying trees by their sapling bark.

Make sure you have permission or a permit to dig in the wild, whether on private property or government land. Landowners may be delighted to have seedlings removed because transplanting can benefit the remaining trees. For example, the ponderosa pine forest in the Black Hills is often not thinned enough, resulting in problems with insects and wildfire. When I remove young trees from my father's timberland, I'm helping, not harming. The same can be true in other areas, but use good judgment to ensure that you are indeed improving things.

My last choice for planting stock is ordering from a commercial nursery because I've had variable quality and success from using their stock. This is not surprising since such catalogs are mailed all over the nation and are not specifically marketed to dryland tree growers.

It's difficult to determine the quality by looking at pictures of perfect specimens in a catalog. If you're unfamiliar with a company, place a small order and evaluate their stock before you send a big check for an entire shelterbelt of trees. Most companies are eager to help you determine if their stock is adapted to your area, and many even offer customer service over the phone.

Planting Techniques

When you plant a tree, you're completing a transplanting process that is extremely stressful to the seedling, especially bare-root stock. When it was dug up from the nursery, it left behind some of its tiny feeder roots and all of the soil that it called home. The moss that keeps the roots damp during shipment is no substitute for the nurturing it received from the earth.

Good planting techniques are especially important in a dryland situation because growing conditions are far from gentle. Don't further cripple an already vulnerable plant by making it start out crammed into a shallow, dry hole. Poor planting is like kicking the injured when they're down. Give young trees the best possible start.

Many seedlings die before they even reach the planting site. The bundle of trees you receive for planting has been out of the ground for quite some time, stressed by heat and drying out during shipment. You can do them their first favor by getting them back in the ground as soon as possible. If you can't plant immediately due to weather conditions, keep the roots cool and moist. They will store a week or more at temperatures of 34° to 38° F with humidity above 90 percent in a root celler or even a refrigerator. The survival rate plummets if the buds break before the trees are planted; these cool temperatures are intended to keep them dormant. If it is still not possible to plant the trees even after a week, dig a trench, spread the seedlings' roots out in it, and cover them with soil to the same depth as they grew in the nursery. The following spring they can be dug up and planted.

Bare-root seedlings should be exposed to sun and wind as little as possible between removing them from packing bundles and planting. Evergreen roots are especially susceptible to damage from sun and wind. Remember that dry roots mean dead trees. On the other hand, drowned roots mean the same thing. Don't soak them for more than a few hours.

Remove only as many trees as you can plant in an hour or two from the shipping bundles so that the rest can stay cool and moist. The roots should be covered with peat moss, moist burlap, or plastic. I used to mix a mud slurry and submerge the roots in it while I'm transporting them to the planting location. The mud coats the roots and keeps them from drying during planting. After I've dug a hole, I pull one tree at a time from the bucket.

An even more effective way to protect roots is use of finely ground, cross-linked polyacrylamide powder mixed with water to create a honey-like, clinging gel. This is the same product that is used in crystal form to provide seedlings a store of water in the planting hole. It absorbs water and releases it later to the roots. In the future it is likely that nurseries will dip roots of seedlings in this gel seconds after they're lifted from the soil. This way the roots aren't exposed to drying air. I mix a bucket of this product when I receive my tree order and dip the entire bundle before planting.

The same planting principles apply whether you are planting with a machine or by hand. The object is not just to get the roots into the ground but to restore their natural growing position as much as possible. Root lengths may vary from 6 to 18 inches; planting holes should match the size of the roots. An old cliché says to dig a five-dollar hole for a fifty-cent tree; it's a good idea. Particularly in hard soil, deep tillage and digging a hole larger than the actual root size encourages them to spread out. There should be no twists or balls in the roots. They should be positioned pointing downward and outward, not in a "J" shape. Figure 6.1 shows the way not to plant trees as well as the proper way.

Plant the trees as close as possible to the same depth that they grew in the nursery. You can detect this depth because the color of the stem changes at the previous soil line. If you can't see this line, just make sure that all tiny roots are in the ground. Foliage or needles should never be covered with soil. Keep rocks, leaves, sticks, clods, and even snow out of the planting hole because these prevent good contact between roots and soil. Damp mineral soil should firmly surround the tree roots.

Once you've planted the seedlings it's time to do the watering, mulching, weeding, and cultivating mentioned in the earlier chapters. If you consider these steps as part of the planting process, you are more likely to do them. You'll be tired after the last tree is planted, but it's better to complete the trees' initial care than neglect it until it's too late. You can't rely on hit or miss methods to grow trees. Such practices generally result in hit-or-miss trees, too. None of the methods that I've outlined are optional. Plant trees the right way, and they will thank you with good growth and a long life.

Evergreens need special care in order to survive. A conifer is not dormant like a deciduous tree is at planting time. It continues to transpire, losing moisture through its needles, even during shipment and while it struggles to become established in its new growing situation. When we planted our first

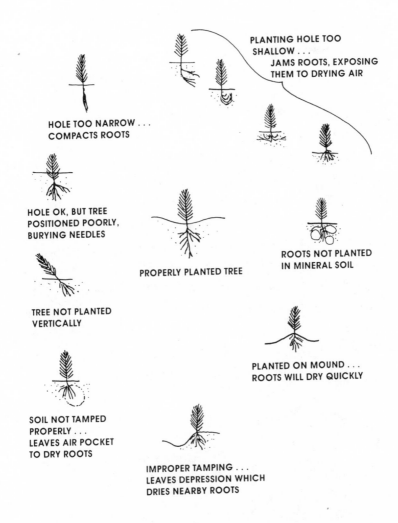

PLANTING HOLE TOO SHALLOW . . . JAMS ROOTS, EXPOSING THEM TO DRYING AIR

HOLE TOO NARROW . . . COMPACTS ROOTS

HOLE OK, BUT TREE POSITIONED POORLY, BURYING NEEDLES

PROPERLY PLANTED TREE

ROOTS NOT PLANTED IN MINERAL SOIL

TREE NOT PLANTED VERTICALLY

PLANTED ON MOUND . . . ROOTS WILL DRY QUICKLY

SOIL NOT TAMPED PROPERLY . . . LEAVES AIR POCKET TO DRY ROOTS

IMPROPER TAMPING . . . LEAVES DEPRESSION WHICH DRIES NEARBY ROOTS

Fig. 6.1. Good and poor examples of tree plantings.

shelterbelt, we included Rocky Mountain juniper, but only six have survived. Most didn't make it through the first summer. The broadleaf trees had the same care and they are doing well. Obviously, the same care is not enough.

I spray my evergreen seedlings with a commercial anti-transpirant preparation that coats the needles and prevents excessive moisture loss. It's the same type of product that is sprayed on Christmas trees to keep them fresh longer. This is effective on newly planted evergreens because their roots often can't take in moisture as fast as the needles are transpiring, so this spray solution slows the outgo until the roots improve their intake.

Never let evergreen roots dry out that first year after transplanting. Keep weeds under control and water as needed. Once the needles start to turn brown it's too late. Shade and protection from hot, dry winds are important to the survival of conifers. Position wooden shingles or old boards on the sides of the tree that get the hottest winds of summer. In our area the wind is out of the southwest on the scorching days, so that is the wind I need to protect my conifers from. Leave the other sides open. (See Figure 6.2.) The boards should be set so that shade is provided from just after midday throughout the afternoon. This keeps the tree cooler so it won't transpire at a rapid rate. Leave the shade and wind protection in place for at least the first year and more if the tree has a poor color. No harm will come by leaving the shade in place longer than one year as long as it's not obstructing the tree's growth.

Fig. 6.2. Wooden shingles protect conifer seedlings.

Protection from Animals

Proper dryland growing techniques are critical in keeping trees alive on the plains, but they're not the only factor. Protecting trees from animal damage is essential. Animals and trees are not a good mixture. All tree plantings must be protected from browsing, grazing, rooting, nibbling, rubbing, marking territory, and soil compaction from pounding hooves. Cattle and horses rub and graze; pigs dig and eat tree roots; sheep, deer, and goats browse tender shoots and strip bark; cottontails, jackrabbits, and mice nibble young tree bark in winter; porcupines even eat the bark of mature trees; dogs urinate on trees and damage evergreens especially; chickens peck new shoots and scratch up a dust bath in the soil that nurtures tiny feeder roots.

Cattle will rub down even large bushes and young trees, ruining the lower density of an entire shelterbelt. This will make it less effective in stopping snow for its own moisture needs and for protecting home and property. Cattle compact the soil beneath trees, which shuts off the supply of water and oxygen.

Although animals aren't going to harm your summerfallowed ground, there is good reason to erect the fence before you plant. Once your trees arrive in the spring, your time will be occupied with planting, mulching, watering, and cultivating on top of your normal activities. Little time will remain then for putting up fence. Keeping animals out of trees is too important to put off.

Most critters can be fenced out with stout posts and three or four strands of barbed wire. Woven wire on the bottom portion of the fence is effective in keeping smaller animals out. While you're building fence, you may as well build it so that it will last a long time. Livestock should never be allowed access to your trees, even when the trees are fully grown. Trees that are planted for the purpose of protecting stock still should be fenced. The protected area in the lee of the trees is where the stock should be, not loafing and rubbing within the shelterbelt rows. (See Figure 6.3.)

Situate the fence so that it allows adequate room to cultivate around the outer rows of a shelterbelt. If some other form of weed control is used, put the fence far enough away from the trees so that cattle cannot reach across and prune the tips off your trees.

Erecting protective structures around individually grown trees is a job that must be done after the tree is planted. Structures keeping out small animals are too small to allow a spade to maneuver inside for planting. It's just as important, however, to protect a tree growing solo from animal damage as it is an entire shelterbelt.

It is time consuming to construct a separate fence for each individual tree, but if it is growing where stock has access, that is what needs to be done. I've used wooden pallets that lumber yards throw away to protect lone trees growing in a pasture, for instance. Four or five of them wired onto posts set in a circle around the tree provide adequate protection from stock.

Mulched trees are subject to mouse damage because the mulch provides a dandy mouse condo. Pulling the mulch away from the trunks will help, but protecting each trunk with aluminum foil is more effective against both mice

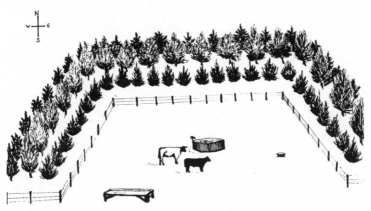

Fig. 6.3. Windbreak for livestock protection.
Note the presence of water, salt, and feed facilities within the
protection of the windbreak.

and rabbits. Used foil is perfectly good for this purpose, and rodents will not chew through it.

If small critters are going to be your only problem with individually grown trees, they can be fenced away with a circle of small mesh chicken wire or hardware cloth. Be sure to bury it in the soil to prevent hungry rabbits from crawling under it to dine on your seedlings.

Individual tree shelters that I've already mentioned are also an excellent way to eliminate small animal damage. I've not tried them to prevent deer and cattle damage, but the 4- and 6-foot-size shelters are said to be effective.

Another new product coming onto the market is a tablet of extremely bitter substance that you drop into the hole at planting time. It is a water-soluble material, so the roots absorb it and carry the bitterness to the leaves. Any animal tasting the tree quickly changes its mind about taking another bite. The product is still in preliminary testing stages as yet and not widely available, but look for it on the market.

Renovation

Renovation starts with a good tree planting design because your planning can avoid problems in the future. A Soil Conservation Service specialist or extension agent can help you with this important preliminary work. Emphasize to this person that you want your tree planting designs to be appropriate to our dry climate. Allow plenty of room between trees and rows for cultivation and for the trees to obtain moisture. If you are growing trees on a high and dry spot, don't even consider water-loving trees. Plant the kinds of trees that survive droughts and harsh conditions, and much renovation will be unnecessary.

Not every tree lives, even with the best of care. Replanting trees that have failed and the renovation of tree plantings must be a continual process, starting with the replacement of dieouts the spring after planting. No matter how good the care you provide your trees, you will not have 100 percent survival. Dead trees need to be replaced; otherwise, you are promoting the failure of the planting from the beginning. It is easier to replace trees when the whole population is young. Mature trees may have their water-seeking roots in place where you plant a replacement and make it difficult for young trees to establish themselves and survive easily.

Remember that an effective shelterbelt has no gaps; dead seedlings mean gaps later on. Take inventory late in the summer of the year you plant your trees and plan to order enough to replace those that are dead. I order a somewhat larger size seedling for replacement stock than I purchased for the original planting so that they will be as effective as those first planted. Be absolutely certain that your replacements are a good, tough variety; perhaps the original selections failed because they were not.

Chances are that sometime in your tree-growing career, you're going to have an entire shelterbelt or other planting with too high a percentage of dead trees to be effective. When a tree planting is no longer doing the job for which it was intended, the investment of time and resources is not paying a return and the planting needs to be returned to usefulness.

A good shelterbelt for snow and wind protection is tall, dense, and continuous. Those that have gaps and poor density need repair work. When entire species die out, gaps are created contributing to the decline in the vigor of the entire planting. Such a lack of vitality makes the crowns thin and impairs the trees' ability to trap snow for their own moisture needs. Each weakening effect leads to another until the shelterbelt or planting is a sad sight.

A cause for poor growth always exists. A shelterbelt's decline is a reaction to stress: insect attack, disease, animals, aging trees, herbicides, lack of a snow-catching shrub row, drought, crowding of trees, or competition from weeds and grasses. Sometimes it is the accumulation and interaction of several stresses that finally cause a shelterbelt to collapse. One stress, such as lack of moisture due to weed growth, may open the door for insect problems. The degree of stress that the trees are under can roughly be determined by what is growing amid the trees. If weeds grow between the rows, the planting is currently under stress. If grass had sodded over the entire shelterbelt, it has been under stress for quite some time.

While these stresses create problems in tree plantings, the removal of the causal stress usually leads to improvements. An extension service tree specialist can help you determine what the problem is in your planting and evaluate the best course of action. Perhaps the answer is as simple as a better fence to keep livestock out or improved weed control. If the trees are reaching the end of their natural life span, the best plan may be to plant additional rows on either side of the existing planting. This way, the old planting can still give what protection it can while the new planting is growing.

Renovation is a continuous process. It's a matter of paying attention to what is happening among your trees and doing all you can to ensure that each tree has optimum growing conditions. Each one influences the success of the entire planting.

Our own shelterbelts are examples of constant renovation. We have continually replaced dieouts. Since so few of the original junipers survive in our first shelterbelt, any replacements we make there are pine or juniper. We may add rows of evergreens to the windward side to increase snow storage and winter density. This would create an even better cattle protection area. Eventually we may have to remove alternate rows so that we can continue cultivation.

It sounds scientific to say "assess the condition of your trees"; in reality, it's only a matter of a pleasant summer evening's walk among them, enjoying the fragrance of Russian olives while you note how much growth they've put out. You can look for borer damage in your green ash trees while trying to find the northern oriole nests in their branches. When you compare heights of your kids versus the pine trees, you can also check for pine tip moth in the growing tips. When you're harvesting chokecherries for jelly, you can be on the lookout for insect webs in the boughs.

Bill and I have labored over our trees together, planting, cultivating, weeding, and watering. Appropriately, some of our most enjoyable times have been spent appreciating our trees. Sometimes we just need a "tree break" and take a walk among our trees to survey our kingdom together. We feel pride in how well our trees have grown and often use our tree walks to compare and evaluate various growing methods that we've used. Always, we are plotting new plans for still more trees.

The most important piece of tree growing advice is this: don't give up. Keep trying to grow trees. Plant some every year without fail. You may plant trees in some terrifically dry years and have to work hard to preserve them, but by planting every year, you'll also hit the years that set high rainfall records and make your tree growing easy. Always be on the lookout for better ideas in tree care. If you're having a tough time getting evergreens established, for example, keep trying while searching for better methods than the ones that failed. Planting a tree is one thing you'll never be sorry you did.

It's a good idea to think big and start small. In other words, design a tree planting that includes all the trees you may ever want to plant. You need not plant them all in one year. If your site is a particularly windy one, it will be difficult to get trees—notably evergreens—established, so it is a good idea to start with easy-to-grow species such as Siberian elm. As these grow quickly and begin to slow the wind, more difficult-to-grow species can be planted. Remember, plant only what you can care for. But plant!

CHAPTER SEVEN

The Value of Trees

Why should I plant trees? I love the plains. I love to top a rise and see a mirage on the horizon 30 miles away. In autumn the grasses turn more delicate shades of tan, gray-green, and rust than even Charlie Russell could paint. I like the looks of cattle with their heads down, grazing hillsides of buffalo grass. I appreciate being able to see stars right down to the horizon and company coming up the road a mile away.

Much as I like all those things, there are aspects of the plains that I would like to change: the wind is number one on my list. It deposits snowdrifts on the road and in the corrals; it takes soil from my garden and filters it through my laundry on the clothesline. Anyone who has lived on the plains knows the wind's reputation for rearranging freshly made haystacks, piling tumbleweeds against the fence, and burying fences in topsoil. The wind is a part of our environment, but it needs to be controlled to make the plains more comfortable. Trees are an excellent way to tame the wind without taking away any of the things that we already like about our land.

I am convinced that more trees would be an asset on the plains, but some may say that planting a tree in a grassland ecosystem interferes with the delicate balance in the same way that cutting down trees in a rain forest has repercussions beyond the tropical environment. Should we plant trees on the plains? After all, it took thousands of years to evolve the grass mix and ecology of the plains. There exists a delicate relationship among thin and often alkaline topsoil, plant species, wind, humidity, moisture or lack of it, extremes in temperatures, high evaporation, diversity of insects, and animals domestic or wild. Should we interfere?

Our very presence on the planet and the plains impacts our environment. Most, but probably not all, of those repercussions are necessary for our survival. We accept having to do some harmful things, so it seems morally right that we balance with positive impacts as well. Trees are perhaps the single most important way to soften the effects of human existence.

For instance, we are willing to plow up prairie land and plant wheat. The wisdom of this is debated from the halls of Congress to the cafes of our home towns; it was especially debated when the wheat fields, borne by the winds in the 1930s, actually reached the halls of Congress. What came out of that crisis was not a moratorium on wheat farming. On the contrary, the great shelterbelt planting movement of the 1930s and 1940s followed. Between 1935 and 1942, 222 million shelterbelt trees were planted in what was known as the Prairie States Forestry Project. From North Dakota to Texas, 18,600 miles of field windbreaks were planted. The first shelterbelt of that era was an Austrian pine planting in

Oklahoma in 1935. It is still alive and well today, creating a positive impact to balance a negative one.

Should we interfere with nature by planting trees on the plains? Do we dare not? It is true that the Great Plains is a unique and valuable ecosystem, and we do not want to give up any of those good things. My father defended our dry South Dakota land like this, "We don't want to make this country just like the east. We can't grow corn or trees like they can, but they can't grow western wheatgrass like we can." I love this country as it is, too. It's open and clean and it's good that way. I don't intend for my promotion of tree planting on the plains to be a slur on the value of grassland.

It's difficult to grow trees where it's dry 7/8 of the time. It's discouraging. It's hard work. It's also extremely worthwhile. Few things you can do net so much profit in terms of benefits to the environment, your livestock, wildlife, and your enjoyment of living. Those benefits accrue both in the short term and in the long term; if you're looking for a good investment of time, money, and effort, plant trees.

Some families pass along silverware, clocks and recipes from parents to children; my family passes along trees. My great-great-grandfather cleared land in Wisconsin in the 1800s, but he liked a certain sapling so much that he left it standing in a corner of his field; he was so foresighted that he specified in his will that the tree should remain. His great-grandson honors that will today, and the tree is known as the "grandfather tree." It's an oak and a very nice one, a treasured family heirloom. I hope my descendants don't have their hearts set on silver because I've always hated to polish the stuff. I prefer Russian olives with sharp-tailed grouse grazing on the berries the morning after a snowfall.

Recommended Reading

American Forestry. A journal published by the American Forestry Association.

Barr, Claude A. *Jewels of the Plains*. Minneapolis, Minn.: University of Minnesota Press, 1983.

Oosterhuis, H. T. *Shelterbelt Planting and Farmstead Beautification*. Edmonton, Alberta: Alberta Agriculture, Plant Industry Division, 1986.

Postel, Sandra, and Lori Heise. "Reforesting the Earth." In *World Watch Paper 83*. Washington, D.C.: World Watch Institute, April 1988.

Riffle, Jerry W., and Glenn W. Peterson. *Diseases of Trees in the Great Plains*. USDA Forest Service, General Technical Report RM 129. Fort Collins, Colo.: Rocky Mountain Forest and Range Experiment Station, 1987.

Urban Forest Forum. A journal published by the American Forestry Association.

Woody Ornamentals for the Prairie Provinces. Edmonton, Alberta: University of Alberta, in association with the Manitoba Department of Agriculture, 1975.

Index

Index

Index

1034